MULTI-FAITH
TOPICS
IN THE
PRIMARY SCHOOL

Janice Webb

CASSELL

Cassell Publishers Limited
Villiers House, 41/47 Strand, London WC2N 5JE, England

First published 1990

British Library Cataloguing in Publication Data
Webb, Janice
  Multi-faith topics in the primary school.
  1. Religions.
  I. Title
  291

ISBN 0-304-31772-1

Illustrations by Rodney Sutton
Typeset by Litho Link Limited, Welshpool, Powys, Wales
Printed and bound in Great Britain by the Bath Press, Avon

CONTENTS

To my parents, Frank and Jean Mitchell, and my husband, Robin, for continuing support and encouragement in all I do.

PREFACE

This is a book for the busy primary school teacher who wants to include more about world religions in Religious Education (R.E.) or project work, but hasn't got time to do the extra research to improve her knowledge. It is not another book on the theory of religious education, nor is it a book giving you some inspiration, then leaving it up to you to find the necessary information and resources. It gives you enough information to teach a topic, references for further reading and resources and practical ideas for carrying out the work.

If you want to include aspects of Christianity, Judaism, Islam and Hinduism in your classroom work, then this is the book for you. Whether you already know quite a bit or you know nothing, it doesn't matter. I have not assumed prior knowledge, but have addressed, as they say, 'the intelligent reader'.

The book contains some background information on the above religions and information sufficient to enable you to teach the topics suggested in each chapter. The material can also be approached thematically. For example, Islamic architecture with its geometric shapes might emerge from work in mathematics, the Hindu festival of Diwali might feature in a study on light, and Jewish recipes might be tried out as part of a topic on food. On the other hand, Diwali may be studied for its own sake, Islam could be studied in depth as a major world religion and Jewish worship looked at on its own or alongside Christianity. It depends on you, your class and your favoured approach.

Acknowledgements

The author and publishers wish to thank the following:

The Humanities Faculty at The Grange Comprehensive, Runcorn, particularly Irene Airton, and the R.E. department at The Heath Comprehensive School, Runcorn, for help and inspiration.

The staff and pupils of All Saints C.E. School, Hoole, Chester, especially Janice Ford.

The staff and pupils of Waverton County Primary School, Chester, especially David Craddock.

Robin Webb, Jane Kenyon, Sheila Nicholas and Margaret Gibson for reviewing scripts.

Naomi Kingston of King David Primary School, Liverpool, Cherrie Wilde and Mr Allam for help in my research.

The following items are reproduced by permission:

Stories on pp. 41–2, 108–9 from *Love at Home* by Khurram Murad: The Islamic Foundation;

Recipes on pp. 88–9, 121 from the King David School handbook, Liverpool: King David Foundation; on pp. 77, 97–8 from *Madhur Jaffrey's Indian Cookery* by Madhur Jaffrey: BBC Enterprises Ltd;

Poem on p. 73: J. Copeland on behalf of Caroline Copeland; Illustration on p. 59: the artist, Diana Golledge; Photographs on pp. 29, 119: Jewish Education Bureau; on pp. 34, 53, 87: Council of Christians and Jews; on pp. 44, 62, 95: Indian High Commission; on p. 56: J. Allan Cash Ltd; on p. 61: A. M. Photo Agency; on pp. 68, 101: Liba Taylor.

INTRODUCTION

Why R.E.?

According to the Education Reform Act 1988, schools must provide religious education for all registered pupils. R.E. is in the unique position of being a compulsory subject while not being in the core curriculum. It is also a subject from which parents have the right to withdraw their children. Any syllabus for R.E. should 'reflect the fact that the religious traditions of Great Britain are in the main Christian while taking into account the teaching and practices of the other principal religions'. The themes, information and ideas in this book relate to Christianity and to Judaism, Islam and Hinduism.

Education Reform Act aside, abiding arguments for teaching R.E. are well rehearsed and I do not intend to go into detail here. Suffice it to say that religion permeates our everyday lives. Look in the newspaper, switch on the news. There are stories of Catholics and Protestants in Northern Ireland, Arabs and Muslims in the Middle East, what the Church thinks of government social policies and what the government thinks about the Church's spiritual and moral leadership. Moral issues such as abortion and whether to bring back capital punishment are constantly debated; the arguments are not complete without the contributions of religious leaders. Many of us pass churches and other religious buildings on our way to school and work each day, we read poetry and literature which alludes to religious concepts, we see religious images in art galleries. Most important, we meet people who hold strong religious beliefs, whether or not they are the Christian ones with which we are familiar.

There may be Jewish, Muslim, or Hindu children in our class or our town; there certainly are in Britain and the world at large. Children are truly not educated for life in our pluralist society unless they know something of the religions of the world. With such knowledge, they are more likely to tolerate, even empathise with, people of different beliefs and cultures. We do not hesitate to teach about the geography and history of other countries and we should not fight shy of teaching about religions that have originated in other countries, as well as teaching about Christianity – which of course was also once an import.

Why so young?

Some teachers are reluctant to study religious education with children in the infant school, and are particularly reluctant to introduce them to the several main faiths. One argument in support of this attitude is that the children do not understand their 'own religion' so how will they possibly understand others?

But what really is the situation? Can we assume that the children before us are Christian – that is, if they are not Jews, Muslims, Hindus or Sikhs? Most children are from families who, even if they are nominally Christian, do not attend church, are unsure of their beliefs or adhere to many superstitions. So we cannot assume children are being introduced to Christianity at home.

And what do we mean by 'understand'? How many adults really understand Christianity with all its complexities and biblical contra-dictions? Yet many of us find it easy to teach about Christmas every year, and do not expect infants to grapple with the idea of Jesus as the incarnation of God. Even sixth-formers, and indeed professors of theology and bishops, have trouble with that one. No, we begin in the children's experience of giving and receiving, of the atmosphere of joy at Christmas time and the story of the child born in the stable and we add to it as years go by. Can we not do this with aspects of world religions?

I have chosen topics for this book which are straightforward or which easily find links to children's experience, or to Christian concepts with which they may be familiar: topics such as religious buildings and family life, festivals and harvest. Deeper concepts can be studied within themes, if you feel it would be appropriate.

Some teachers object that as they have no children in their schools other than 'Christians', they do not need to teach anything but Christianity. While I agree that (especially in the case of infants) it helps to have a non-Christian in the class as a spur to investigating another faith and its customs, yet I would argue that since we live in a pluralist society and a multi-cultural world children need some knowledge of world religions in order to make sense of that world. Multi-faith R.E. is as valuable in culturally monochrome areas as it is in areas which boast a diversity of beliefs. In the latter, the resources are easier to obtain and more questions about 'other faiths' might arise naturally. But there is no reason to ignore other faiths if there are no adherents in your class, just as you would not refuse to teach about other countries or about say,

Roman Britain. We often have to introduce children to things outside (but we hope with some relevance to) their experience.

Approaches to teaching R.E.

In recent years, opinion on how to teach R.E. has wavered between the implicit approach and the explicit approach.

The implicit approach begins in the child's experience and moves out to the unknown, for example through the use of what Goldman, in the 1960s, called 'life themes', where explicit material, as long as it is not contrived, can be brought in to illuminate children's first-hand experience. In the 1970s Michael Grimmitt introduced the idea of 'depth themes' which were designed to encourage an understanding of religion, rather than foster a belief in Christianity. Such themes might be homes, light, special occasions, the religious significance of which can be at least partly grasped through the children's own experience and feelings. It is an approach which allows you to move out gradually to more explicit matters concerning chosen world faiths. Perhaps most useful when teaching infants, it is also useful with any age group to demonstrate the relevance of religion to life.

Other possible themes include: friends, neighbours, mothers and fathers, gifts, seasons, journeys, courage, birthdays, caring, colour, myself, books, buildings, initiation, food and hunger and forgiveness. You will find some of these themes put into context in this book.

The explicit approach tends to be Bible-orientated or to present explicit facts about world religions. It involves presenting information in a neutral way and can help to remove ignorance and prejudice against different ways of life. To benefit from this approach learners need to be able to enjoy and digest facts, yet it can be used even with young children to add to their experience of religious festivals and rites of passage, such as birth, initiation, marriage and death.

The approach in this book

I have taken both approaches, according to context. With infants, it is necessary to start in their experience, whether it be following up the questions that naturally arise or working within a selected theme, such as 'light', 'homes' or 'families'. Their experiences can be built upon and the children gently introduced to different ways of life and belief. Indeed, with pupils of any age, using existing experiences and providing new ones in the form of music, poetry, food, visits to people and buildings, help the learner to get the 'feel' of a religion without actually participating in it.

The explicit factual approach is taken whenever giving facts may help children learn about how people do things and what it means to be religious. I think we need to be flexible in our teaching methods and indeed in the broader question of how we provide religious education in the curriculum.

R.E. does not have to appear in a particular 'slot' so that we can say we have 'done our statutory R.E.'. Religion can permeate our curriculum. A project on puppet-making could culminate in acting out a Hindu legend or a Christian parable. A visit to a farm at springtime might encourage wonder at the miracle and cycle of life which in turn might lead to an appreciation of the joy felt by Christians at Easter and Hindus at Holi.

R.E. need not upset the balance of the curriculum. There is no need to feel afraid of 'spending too much time on R.E.' if religion is seen as part of life and studied from different angles or in a broader context. While studying Islamic prayer, which takes place at specified times of the day, children can be aided in learning to tell the time. A study of Diwali can include an appreciation of Indian music and dance – and the children can do their own movement and dance to it. Artistic and dramatic expression can be encouraged in pictorial and theatrical representations of religious stories. Children can practise written work as they describe religious practices and feelings and reproduce legends in their own words. Approached this way, R.E. can be part of a broad cross-curricular theme of multi-culture as well as a discrete subject in accordance with the Education Reform Act.

The plan of this book

Chapter 1 is intended to give you a brief introduction to Judaism, Islam, Christianity and Hinduism and put into context the topics in the subsequent chapters (see p. 27 for suggestions on further introductory reading). Each of the following chapters takes a topic and shows how it can be dealt with in the classroom, starting with background information, then suggesting thematic approaches and possible tasks. These suggestions are not exhaustive. All recipes, poems and prayers are given in full and there are diagrams and instructions where necessary.

Some tasks are labelled Level One and Level Two, levels which broadly correspond to infant and junior, though some can be adapted to either age group. The tasks which have not been labelled in this way can usually be attempted in some degree by either age group.

I have not made many suggestions for written work because you will know best how to tailor such work for each individual in your class.

A word of warning. If there are children of various faiths in your class, think twice about using them as a human resource. Many young children are not as conversant with their religion as we might think and we must beware of making one child look 'different' or 'strange'. You will know whether a child will want to be left alone or be out at the front bursting with pride about his or her religion.

BIBLIOGRAPHY

Derek Bastide, *Religious Education 5–12* (Falmer Press, 1987) (Mayhew-McCrimmon 1982)

R. J. Goldman, *Religious Thinking from Childhood to Adolescence* (Routledge & Kegan Paul, 1964)

R. J. Goldman, *Readiness for Religion* (Routledge & Kegan Paul, 1965)

Michael Grimmitt, *What Can I Do in R.E.?* 2nd ed. (Mayhew-McCrimmon, 1982)

Jean Holm, *Teaching Religion in School* (Oxford University Press, 1975)

Robert Jackson, *Approaching World Religions* (John Murray, 1982)

The Swann Report, *Education for All: A Brief Guide to the Main Points of the Report* (HMSO, 1985)

1 WORLD FAITHS: AN INTRODUCTION

Judaism

Origins

Judaism is the oldest religion in the Western world, but has far fewer adherents than Islam and Christianity. There are only fourteen million Jews in the world, including half a million in Great Britain. However, Judaism is the parent religion to Islam and Christianity and so it has an indirect effect on hundreds of millions of people. Judaism is not a missionary religion although people can be converted to it through a lengthy process of learning and commitment. People born to Jewish mothers are Jews.

Abraham is usually regarded as the founder of Judaism although Jews believe that it was to Moses on Mount Sinai that God revealed the code by which they should live: the Ten Commandments. Abraham lived approximately 4000 years ago when the Hebrews were a semi-nomadic people who worshipped an anonymous God: 'the God of my father'. These people, led by the great patriarchs Abraham, Isaac and Jacob, believed that the land of Canaan was promised to them, but it was with Moses in the thirteenth century B.C. that the history of Israel as a Jewish nation began.

At this time the Hebrews were slaves in Egypt and badly treated by the Pharaoh who would not set them free. Eventually, through a sequence of events beginning with the plagues and ending with the parting of the Red Sea, the Hebrews were able to escape, led by Moses and, they believe, helped by God. After many years of wandering, during which Moses died, they settled in Canaan, later named Israel. It was the laws arising from the commandments revealed by God to Moses and the faith in One God that formed the basis of Judaism during the period of settlement in Israel and into the present day. The Jewish kingdom eventually had its own kings, one of the most famous being David, but the Jews were dispersed in A.D. 70 and were scattered until the establishment of the independent state of Israel in 1948. Many Jews are still scattered throughout the world today and those in Israel live, sometimes uneasily, alongside Muslims and Christians, to whom also Israel, particularly Jerusalem, is a holy place.

Throughout their history, the Jews have been persecuted, most recently and horrifically by command of Hitler in the Holocaust, when six million Jews were slaughtered. Yet in spite of this, and indeed perhaps because of it, the Jews have survived, gaining in strength and deepening their identity.

Holy writings

The Jews' holy book is the Bible, but only the books which Christians refer to as the Old Testament. The first five books, which are known collectively as the Pentateuch, contain the Torah (meaning 'Law' or 'teaching'), and are attributed to Moses; the Psalms to David. The other books can be categorised as prophecy, history and wisdom. Another holy book is the Talmud, a collection of 63 books by 2000 authors, dating from the early Christian era and containing rabbinic interpretations and commentaries on the scriptures. Jews do not believe that holy writings are confined to the past; they are still possible today.

Holy days

The Jewish Sabbath begins at sunset on Friday and ends at sunset on Saturday. Worship takes place both in the synagogue and at home (see pp. 33-4, 52ff. for more details). There are several festivals observed throughout the year both at home and in the synagogue, some of which are dealt with in this book. Often a festival will simultaneously commemorate an incident in Jewish history and celebrate a spiritual meaning, most notably Passover (Pesach), which celebrates the exodus from Egypt and looks forward to peaceful times for the Jews. This hope is summed up in the final words of the Passover celebration:

Peace, Shalom
Peace for us! For everyone!
For all people, this, our hope:
Next year in Jerusalem.
Next year may all be free!

Customs

There are many customs and food laws observed in the Jewish home, dealt with in the chapter on family life (pp. 29ff.). Suffice it to say here that the home life of a Jew is as important, if not more so, as what goes on in the synagogue.

Throughout their lives the Jews are involved in ritual and symbolism to mark special occasions and their whole life revolves around their religion. At eight days of age, a Jewish boy is circumcised in accordance with the Law. After studying Hebrew, Jewish history, scripture and Law for some years he will, at 13, come of age and take his vows as an adult Jew. This ceremony is called Bar Mitzvah, meaning 'son of the Law'. In more liberal strands of Judaism, a similar ceremony is carried out for the girls called Bat Mitzvah (daughter of the Law).

The Reform Jews are more liberal in their thinking and do not necessarily adhere strictly to all of the Laws, particularly those concerning food. The Orthodox Jews observe the letter of the Law more closely and do not recognise as valid some of the practices of Reform Judaism, for example the mode of conversion of Gentiles to Judaism. They call such converts to Judaism proselytes, and regard them as part of their religion, but not of their race.

As in other religions, the ceremonies surrounding death are designed to comfort the bereaved and to treat the departed with as much dignity as possible. The body is washed and wrapped in a white shroud and, for a man, his *tallith* (prayer shawl). Burial should take place the day after death if possible. Cremation is allowed by some Jewish congregations. The first week after death is a time of intense mourning and on the anniversary of death candles are lit in the home of the relatives and a Kaddish (prayer of sanctification) offered in the synagogue.

Beliefs

The main theological tenet of Judaism is the belief in one God as summed up in the opening line of the Shema: 'Hear, O Israel, the Lord our God is *one* Lord' (Deuteronomy 6:4). Ethics and ritual are very important to Jews as they are laid down in the Torah. Bound up in the nature of Judaism is the corporate identity of its people which is social and political as well as religious. Judaism teaches that a person should behave justly and be a good citizen and abhor violence, murder and war. However, killing in self-defence is legitimate as is the execution of dangerous criminals after a fair trial. Abortion is mandatory if there is a threat to the mother's life. Although family life is of paramount importance, divorce is permitted and easy to obtain through the Jewish council, the Beth Din, after a divorce has been granted by civil law. Nonetheless, divorce is regarded as a failure and a cause for mourning.

Islam

Islam is a major world religion. The areas of the world showing the greatest density of Muslims are Pakistan, Bangladesh, Indonesia, Saudi Arabia, Turkey, Iran, Iraq, Egypt, Israel, Morocco, Libya, Tunisia and Algeria. There are around one million Muslims in Great Britain: the largest non-Christian community in the country. Although there has been much immigration into Britain over the past 40 years, Muslims have been resident here since the early nineteenth century. There is a mosque in Woking dating back to 1889.

The word Islam is a verbal noun meaning 'to submit' and, theologically speaking, the word 'commitment' most aptly renders the true meaning. It is a continual commitment to God (Allah), renewed daily as the devout Muslim seeks to know and serve God.

Islam was founded in the seventh century A.D., the usual date given being A.D. 622, denoting the time when Muhammad (Islam's founder) and his Meccan converts settled in Yathrib (later known as Medina) in Arabia. The Muslim calendar is dated from this time. For Muslims our year 1989 is A.H. 1408. There are fewer days in the Muslim year because their months are lunar. Thus the Muslim year gradually works its way through our year and the months which correspond with ours differ each year.

Origins

Muhammad was born about A.D. 570 in Mecca, a prosperous caravan centre between South Arabia and the Mediterranean countries. He was a happily married man and a successful trader. Mecca was a wealthy city partly because much trade was done with the pilgrims who came to worship many gods there. Muhammad began to think about this polytheism and worship of idols. Surely all beliefs could not be right? He also felt it was wrong that some people were rich while others were extremely poor, and that certain cruelties, such as abandoning baby girls in the desert as sacrifices to spirits, could be justified by reference to supernatural beliefs.

As he approached his fortieth year, Muhammad spent much time contemplating these things. One day, as he sat outside the city, he saw a vision. A figure carrying a cloth approached him, commanding Muhammad to read what was written on the cloth. Muhammad was afraid and also aware that he was unable to read. Suddenly he found himself comprehending what was written:

'Read, in the name of the Lord, who has created all things, who created man out of a clot of blood. Recite in the name of the Most High, who has taught man the use of the pen, who teaches man what he did not know.'

When he got home Muhammad told his wife what he had read and they both believed that through this vision he had been called by God to speak out against the idol-worship and polytheism of the people of Mecca and, indeed, of most Arabs in north and central Arabia. Until Muhammad's death Allah continued to communicate with Muhammad through the Angel Gabriel, and his highly educated son-in-law wrote down the words. The result is the Muslims' holy book, the Qur'an.

Muhammad made some progress with his message and even won over some of the prominent citizens of Mecca. However, he also made many enemies because fewer pilgrims meant less trade. Eventually Muhammad was invited to go to Yathrib, an invitation he was almost forced to accept in view of the opposition in Mecca. Yathrib consisted of a group of agricultural villages inhabited by Arabs and Jews. Muhammad formed a political community and attacked caravans going to and from Mecca for seven years, during which time the Jews of Yathrib became irreconcilable opponents and were expelled. However, the bedouins of western and central Arabia were incorporated into the Muslim community and in A.D. 630 Mecca fell to Muslim attack and was purified of its polytheistic idolatry. The cube-shaped ancient sanctuary now known as Ka'aba from the Arabic, meaning 'cube', in the city was dedicated to Allah and became the main pilgrimage shrine of Islam.

Muhammad

Muhammad is not seen by Muslims as divine or supernatural, but rather an ordinary man with a special mission from God. He himself admitted to error and said that he had no power to work miracles. He is regarded as the greatest prophet amongst other great prophets, including Adam, Abraham, Moses and Jesus. Thus Islam is linked with Judeo-Christian traditions.

Holy writings

The Qur'an is regarded as a miracle of Muhammad in the sense that he was God's mouthpiece. It is blasphemy to say that Muhammad was its author, for the Qur'an is believed to have been composed by Allah himself. It is believed that the Angel Gabriel dictated it to him over a period of twenty-three years in a series of visions and that it is the final revelation of God's will. The Qur'an is written in Arabic. Muslims still read it in that language and try to learn it by heart.

Customs

The first words heard by a newborn Muslim baby are the tenets of the Islamic faith which are whispered into his ears along with the phrase, 'Prayer is better than sleep', which demonstrates their priorities. Children are instructed in the Qur'an, first at home with their mother and then at special classes. The Qur'an lays upon the Muslim various duties and prohibitions; for example, Muslims are forbidden to eat the flesh of a pig or to drink wine, to gamble, smoke or commit slander and perjury.

Marriages are often arranged but consent is sought from both parties and, although divorce is disapproved of, it is possible.

Burial takes place as soon as possible after death, the body first having been washed with sweet-smelling soaps and spices and laid in a raised grave with the face turned to the right and towards Mecca.

Further details on some of the above customs can be found in Chapter 2.

Beliefs

The main tenet of Islam is the absolute oneness of God (Allah) and that his truth has been revealed to humans in the Qur'an, which also outlines the various duties that believers must carry out. It may be taken that the God referred to by Muslims is that referred to by Jews and Christians, though there may be debate about the nature and will of God. There are five pillars of faith to which each Muslim adheres:

1. Faith in God (Allah)

This faith is confessed by the repetition of the Word of Witness: 'There is no god but the One God and Muhammad is his messenger.' In this phrase polytheism is denounced and Muhammad exalted to the greatest of the prophets of history.

2. Prayer (Salat)

Prayers must be said at five appointed times of the day and there is a sequence of prayer positions to be followed. Friday is the day for congregational worship in the mosque when there will also be a sermon (see pp. 55ff. for further details).

3. Giving charity (Zakat)

It is up to the conscience of the individual Muslim to decide how much money to give, though a fortieth of one's income is an obligatory minimum requirement. The money is used largely to help the poor.

4. Fasting (Sawm)

The Qur'an makes it obligatory for all Muslims to fast during the hours of daylight during the month of Ramadan. During this time they will study the Qur'an and re-assess their life as a Muslim (see Chapter 7 for

5. Pilgrimage (Hajj)

Devout Muslims must try to make at least one visit to the Ka'aba, a huge cube-shaped shrine in the centre of the great mosque in Mecca, believed to have been built by Abraham and for Muslims the holiest spot on earth because of its associations with Muhammad. Every pilgrim to the Ka'aba wears special clothing to signify equality of rich and poor before God. At the end of the period of pilgrimage, there is a festival called Eid-ul-Adha (also celebrated by people who have not visited Mecca), involving feasting and the ritual sacrifice of animals. Part of the meat is given away to the poor.

Hinduism

Origins

Hinduism is one of the world's oldest religions. It is difficult to define because there is no single code of belief or practice and no known founder. Where Christians, Muslims and Jews can be defined by their beliefs and intentions, Hindus cannot. Hinduism is ethnic in origin as much as it is religious, having been part of the culture of the people who lived in the Indus valley. The Indus valley civilisation of 2000 B.C. had, according to archaeologists, a religion with many of the features of Hinduism: a mother goddess, a god similar to the one now known by Hindus as Shiva, and the revered phallic symbols. Certain animals, such as the bull, and certain trees, such as the pipal, were sacred. The pipal is still honoured in both Hinduism and Buddhism. Stress was laid on the importance of ablutions, which accords with modern Hindu custom.

Around the middle of the second millennium B.C., the Indus valley was invaded by a group of tall, fair-skinned people called Aryans, whose major gods were male. Many of the deities they worshipped were nature spirits such as Agni, the god of fire, Indra, the god of the sky, and Varuna, the lord of the waters. The Aryans composed many hymns for use at sacrifices and had a priestly system. Some of these hymns remain in the most ancient and sacred book of the Hindu scriptures, the Rig Veda. The beliefs and practices of the Aryans and Indus valley people were absorbed into one another and new religious philosophies emerged, giving, by 800 B.C., a well-established Hindu religion.

Many of the gods worshipped in those ancient times now have little standing with Hindus. The great warrior god of the Aryans, Indra, has degenerated to a mere rain god, and Varuna, who meted out punishment to men, is remembered only as a sort of Indian Neptune.

Beliefs

There are probably over 400 million Hindus in the world, and amongst them there are so many different beliefs and practices that pass for Hinduism that it is possible for next-door neighbours to worship different gods in different ways and still agree that they are both Hindus. What makes Hinduism so different from the Judaism-based religions is its polytheistic nature, although more modern philosophical Hinduism holds that all gods are but facets of the one great God, often known as Brahman. In the nineteenth-century, the Hindu philosopher Sri Ramakrishna (1836–86) said: 'Different creeds are but different paths to the one God' (saying no. 463). This means that whichever god is particularly worshipped by a family or village, it is the ultimate God who is the recipient.

Hinduism, being such an ancient religion, carries with it some primitive aspects as well as the highly developed philosophical systems. There are some particular features, however, which characterise Hinduism generally. One such is the doctrine of transmigration of souls, which maintains that the soul inhabits many different bodies before reaching its final goal. The behaviour (*karma*) of a person plays a large part in determining the destination of the soul and the body (person or animal) into which it is born next time. Some Hindu sects have absorbed Buddhist ideas with the ultimate goal being a state of *nirvana*. Others, perhaps influenced by Christianity, see a form of salvation at work in the achievement of the ultimate release from the continual cycle of rebirth (*samsara*). Yoga plays its part in the contemplative, ascetic strand of Hinduism that subjugates the body and controls the mind until the soul reaches a higher consciousness.

The major gods of Hinduism make up a triumvirate (*trimurti*) with Brahman (creator), Shiva (the destroyer) and Vishnu (the preserver). All things, seasons and souls, go in cycles with birth following death and these phenomena are in the power of the three main gods. Vishnu is the god most like the Christian concept of God and appears in several incarnations (avatars), the most famous being his incarnations as Rama and Krishna.

There are many others of the ancient gods who are still popular or who are worshipped at particular times. They include Hanuman (the monkey god); Ganesha, the god with the head of an elephant, who is meant to bring good luck to new ventures; Agni, the god of fire; and Lakshmi, the goddess of prosperity.

Holy writings

There are many Hindu scriptures, the Rig Veda, completed by about 900 B.C., being the oldest of them. Many primitive gods are mentioned, some connected with the elements, but towards the end of this hymnal there is evidence of a development in religious outlook particularly concerning the creation of the world. New vedas were written concerning ritual sacrifice (Sama Veda), instructions for the officials at ceremonies (Yajur Veda) and spells for curing diseases (Atharva Veda). Later they were expounded upon in the *Brahmanas*, texts of priestly origin concerned with the minutiae of the sacrificial system.

The Upanishads were probably composed between 800 and 400 B.C. by members of the warrior caste. They mark the end of the Vedic period of writing and the starting point of religio-philosophical thinking in Hinduism. The writings deal largely with the concept of transmigration of the soul (*atman*) and of its release (*moksha*) from this cycle through unity with the absolute, Brahman, who pervades and underlies the cosmos.

The great Hindu epics, the *Mahabharata* and the *Ramayana*, concern two incarnations (avatars) of Vishnu – Krishna and Rama respectively. In the *Mahabharata*, there are long sections giving instructions on ethics, politics, religion and morality. One section, the *Bhagavad-gita*, which takes the form of a dialogue between the warrior, Arjuna, and the Lord Krishna, is concerned with showing God's love for humans and describing a Hindu's duty.

Customs

The caste system is a major characteristic of Hindu life. It is bound up with the concept of *samsara* in that people can be re-incarnated in a higher or lower caste depending upon their actions in life. The highest caste consists of Brahmins – authorities on religious ritual and spiritual and intellectual matters. Next come Kshatriyas, warriors and rulers, followed by Vaishyas, men of commerce, bankers and merchants. The fourth group, called Shudras, are the labourers. Beneath this comes an outcast group (Pariahs), also referred to as 'untouchables', who were renamed Harijans (people of God) by Mahatma Gandhi. Each caste has its own duties and people are supposed to marry within their own caste. Nowadays there is generally less rigidity with regard to the caste system and people may take up any job for which they are trained. It is a punishable practice to regard any person as 'untouchable' and treat them as such.

Worship in the home is important to Hindus and many families will have a home shrine dedicated to a god where they worship daily.

Christianity

Origins

Christianity has its origins in Judaism, since Jesus himself was a Jew, as were his disciples. The word 'Christian' was first coined by non-Christians as a name for the people who believed in a certain Jesus Christ. The term only appears three times in the New Testament, but was eventually used by the believers themselves as they became distinct from the Jews.

Jesus, a Jew from Nazareth in Galilee, Palestine, is generally regarded as the founder of Christianity, but the writings of Paul and the Fourth Gospel have played a major part in shaping Christian theology.

As well as being influenced by Jewish thought and symbolism, early Christianity was also influenced by contemporary Greek philosophy. The spread of Christianity in the first centuries after Christ was helped by Roman roads and postal systems and the fact that its greatest missionary, St Paul, as a Roman citizen, could move freely (most of the time) throughout the vast Roman Empire.

Holy writings

The holy book of Christianity is the Bible and Christians believe it to contain the inspired word of God. The Bible is a compilation of 66 books, 39 of which comprise the Old Testament, also sacred to the Jews, and 27 the New Testament. In this are accounts of the life, works and teachings of Jesus, considered by Christians to be a fulfilment of Judaism and, indeed, to supersede it.

The four Gospels in the New Testament give accounts of the life, works and teachings of Jesus, and also offer a degree of interpretation. Until they were written down, the miracles and teachings of Jesus were told from memory and passed on to believers orally. Mark's gospel is generally thought to be the first written gospel and most scholars believe that the other gospel writers used Mark as a source. The gospels are followed by the book of Acts, which describes the beginnings of the early church and the missionary journeys of St Paul, who took the message to the Gentiles as well as the Jews. The rest of the New Testament consists of letters (epistles), mainly from Paul to the churches he founded, but also from Peter, James and John.

The earliest written account of the Last Supper and Jesus's resurrection is in Paul's first letter to the Corinthians, written about A.D. 52.

Jesus

Born in Bethlehem of the pious Jews, Mary and Joseph, during the reign of Herod the Great, Jesus grew up in Nazareth and followed his father's occupation as a carpenter. Christians believe that Mary was a virgin when she conceived and gave birth to Jesus and that he was the Son of God biologically as well as spiritually.

Jesus's public ministry took place between A.D. 27 and 29. It was heralded by the teaching of John the Baptist – 'The man who comes after me is much greater than I am . . . I baptise you with water, but he will baptise you with the Holy Spirit' (Mark 1:7-8, *Good News Bible*). The whole baptism of Jesus was seen as God's blessing upon Jesus at the start of his ministry. The forty days which followed when Jesus struggled, successfully, in the desert to resist temptations suggested to him by the devil can be seen as his self-abnegation and surrender to his father's will, as well as his preparation for his 'mission'.

Jesus moved around Galilee and the neighbouring districts of Palestine where, according to Christian tradition, he healed the sick, raised the dead, taught about morality and the Kingdom of God. The Jewish idea of this Kingdom was of a golden age of divine blessings for the faithful when a deliverer (Messiah) descended from the great Jewish King, David, would restore the independence the Jews enjoyed during his reign. Jesus was associated with this Messianic figure and, when Peter (Mark 8:29) said: 'You are the Messiah', Jesus did not deny it. He did, however, charge his disciples to keep quiet about it. Jesus was not the sort of Messiah that most Jews of the day (and indeed today) were expecting and ultimately they rejected him and called for his death on a charge of blasphemy. Jesus's teaching on the Kingdom of God was also unexpected. He spoke not of an earthly kingdom but a spiritual one – one which had already begun in the hearts and minds of his followers and which would be fulfilled in the future.

Jesus chose twelve disciples to help him and after Peter's confession, his teaching began to emphasise humility and suffering reminiscent of the text of Isaiah 53, which many see as an Old Testament prophecy of Jesus's mission. Eventually Jesus came into conflict with the Jewish authorities, who pronounced the sentence of death on him and passed him to the Roman governor, Pontius Pilate, who had the authority to order the execution. The night before his arrest, Jesus ate with the disciples and from this time the breaking of bread and sharing of wine took on a new significance for them and subsequently for all Christian believers. The bread and wine have come to symbolise Jesus's body and blood, and his death is seen as a sacrifice marking the start of a new covenant with God.

Jesus's death is not regarded by Christians today as a tragedy or even a martyrdom, but a triumphant event which fulfilled the divine purpose. According to the Gospel writers, Jesus's tomb was found to be empty on the third day and Jesus appeared to various believers at different times before finally ascending to heaven (Acts 1:7-9). Although the Gospel accounts of these events are conflicting and it is not entirely clear whether a spiritual or physical resurrection was meant, the early Christians had no doubt in proclaiming that Jesus was alive, and boldly preached this message.

Paul

St Paul was born Saul, a devout Jew and native of Tarsus in Cilicia. He was well educated, knew Greek and was a Roman citizen. His first contact with Christians was as their persecutor, but his dramatic conversion on the road to Damascus (Acts 9) made him Christianity's greatest missionary and early theologian. Paul took the gospel to the Gentiles and persuaded early church leaders that these Gentile Christians need not observe the Jewish laws of diet and circumcision. It was soon after this that the break from Judaism came and Christianity became a religion in its own right rather than a Jewish sect. Paul completed three missionary journeys, was imprisoned for his faith many times and was probably executed.

Beliefs

Christians believe, much as has been described above, that Jesus was divine, the Son of God, born of the virgin Mary, that he came back to life after his crucifixion and that his Holy Spirit is available to all believers who have repented of their sins, to help them become more like him, to continue his work on earth and finally to be with him in heaven.

Christians, while having few rules about food and none about dress, do follow a strict moral code. It is based on the first two commandments, which Jesus summarised in Mark 12:30 to 31, 'Love the Lord your God with all your heart, with all your soul, with all your mind and with all your strength . . . . Love your neighbour as yourself.' Jesus's teaching, particularly in the parables and the Sermon on the Mount (Matthew 5 to 7) illustrates these commands and deals with specific issues such as forgiveness and divorce.

Sects

Broadly speaking, Christianity is divided into Roman Catholic, Orthodox and Protestant but there are divisions within Protestantism and there are sects, such as Christian Science, which fall outside these main categories.

The Roman Catholics emphasise their continuity with one of Jesus's leading disciples, Peter, who became the first bishop of Rome. The authority over the see of Rome was passed down the generations and the name Pope was given to the holder of the office. In the Middle Ages the Orthodox Churches of the East became separated from Rome. Until the period of the Reformation, broadly the fifteenth to seventeenth centuries, Britain was Roman Catholic but there was much dissension against Rome, particularly over Latin services, the papal rule, priestly celibacy, the doctrine of transubstantiation, and corrupt practices, such as the sale of 'indulgences', where priests offered God's pardon to a sinner in exchange for money. Many new protestant sects sprang up and, under Henry VIII, Britain split from Rome and the Church of England was established. Now the monarch is the head of the Church of England and the top spiritual and pastoral post is that of the Archbishop of Canterbury. Denominations such as Methodists, Baptists and United Reformed Churches are separate from the state and differ with the Church of England over such matters of mode of worship, baptism of infants and general organisation.

Festivals

The main Christian festivals are Easter, celebrating the resurrection of Jesus, Christmas, to celebrate his birth, and Pentecost (often called Whitsuntide) which commemorates the giving of the Holy Spirit to the disciples in Jerusalem about six weeks after the Resurrection. Other festivals include Lent, the six weeks preceding Easter where the theme of self-denial is in sympathy with Jesus resisting temptations in the wilderness, harvest, Mothering Sunday and Epiphany.

Customs

In the majority of Christian Churches babies are baptised to show that they are part of the Christian family and at the baptism the parents and godparents promise to bring the children up as Christians. Amongst Baptists and Pentecostals only adult baptism is observed so that the candidate can truly be said to have chosen the Christian way for himself. This is sometimes called believers' baptism and corresponds more closely with the baptism described in the New Testament even down to complete immersion in the water.

In the Church of England, those who were baptised as babies can come forward to be confirmed as Christians at an age when they are able to choose their religion for themselves. This is often at the age of 13 or 14 or older. Catholics have a similar confirmation and Methodists have a Church membership ceremony.

Marriage for Christians takes place in a church and is regarded by Roman Catholics and the Church of England as a sacrament – a sign of the promise the couple make to each other before God. As such it cannot be broken and civil divorce is not recognised by Roman Catholics, though in the Church of England a more lenient view may be taken in certain circumstances.

Death is followed by burial or cremation with a simple service. Christians take comfort from the biblical promises that after death they will join God in heaven.

Church services are held on a Sunday and include services of communion or eucharist, which recall the Last Supper of Jesus and his disciples with the bread and wine symbolising the body and blood of Jesus. It is a time of thanksgiving for Jesus's sacrifice for them. Most services include hymns of praise to God, readings from the Bible, prayers and a sermon from someone in authority in the church.

BIBLIOGRAPHY

General

The Concise Encyclopedia of Living Faiths, ed. R. C. Zaehner (Hutchinson/
Open University, 1959)
The World Religions (Lion, 1982)
Leonard and Carolyn Wolcott, *Religions Around the World* (Collins, 1970)

Christianity

The New International Dictionary of the Christian Church, ed. J. D. Douglas
(Paternoster, 1974)
The Oxford Dictionary of the Christian Church, ed. F. L. Cross and E. A.
Livingstone (Oxford University Press, 1974).

Judaism

Morris Epstein, *All About Jewish Holidays and Customs* (KTAV Publishing
House, 1959, 1970)
Harry Gersh, *When a Jew Celebrates* (Behrman House, 1971)

Islam

Alfred Guillaume, *Islam* (Penguin, 1954, reprinted several times to 1979)
Richard Tames, *Approaches to Islam* (John Murray, 1982)

Hinduism

The Sayings of Sri Ramakrishna (Amra Press, 1965)
K. M. Sen, *Hinduism* (Pelican, 1961)
Margaret Stutley, *Hinduism* (Aquarian Press, 1985)
Eric J. Sharpe, *Thinking about Hinduism* (Lutterworth, new ed. 1988).

2 FAMILY LIFE

Family life is an important aspect of any culture. The way a family is run will depend on tradition, circumstances and religious beliefs. A family's morals, activities and customs will be linked to their religion and adhering to them helps to preserve their identity.

The way in which, say, a Muslim family can observe traditions and rituals in Britain will differ from their observance in Bangladesh, because the societies are organised so differently. However, there are certain practices that can be carried out in the home wherever in the world a Muslim family may be. Similarly, in the dispersions following persecution, the Jews have retained their identity by continuing their customs in the home.

The most instantly observable aspects of home life for Hindus, Muslims and Jews are food and dress, but the home is important in teaching the children, worshipping and marking special religious events.

Using this chapter

The whole of this chapter, or aspects of it, could be used to support a theme study about homes and families. The children could begin by looking at their own homes and any rituals they may have, such as special Sunday lunches, ways of celebrating birthdays, bedtime routines and so on. Family is important in Christianity and is especially celebrated at Christmas. There will probably be great variations within the class and this could lead to looking at family life in other cultures or religions. It is up to you, the teacher, taking account of the ages and abilities of the children in your class, to decide how many to use of the three examples given here. You could also, if you wished, pursue a historical link here by looking at how people used to live, with the emphasis on extended family groups as well as the lack of household gadgetry we have today.

Alternatively, the information and ideas in this chapter could be used with information from other chapters to construct a study of a particular religion. For instance, the material on Islam in this chapter could be used with the information on Islamic worship in Chapter 3 and on Ramadan in Chapter 7 for a project on Islam. The material on Judaism and ideas for tasks in this chapter could be used in part as an introduction to the festival of Purim (Chapter 5).

Judaism

Home life plays a very important part in Judaism, and the mother of the household is the linchpin in organising the practicalities in the home. It is she who has to take responsibility for whether it will be a truly Jewish (kosher) home or not. As the rabbis said, 'Whatever blessing dwells in the home comes from the wife'.

Every time there is a festival, there is a celebration in the home as well as in the synagogue and the Friday night Sabbath meal is every bit as important as the congregational services on Friday evening and Saturday morning. Apart from these times of specific celebration, every day involves the Jewish wife in upholding the practices of Judaism when she keeps a kosher kitchen.

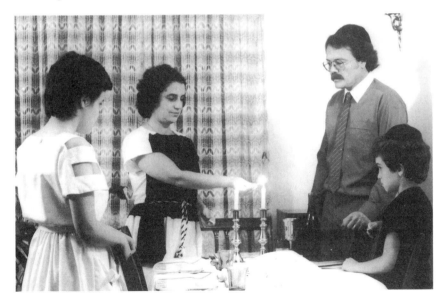

Lighting the Sabbath candles.

Mezuzah

The first thing that you would notice about a Jewish household is the *mezuzah*. This is a small case made out of wood or silver, or other precious metal, attached to the right-hand doorpost of the house. There may be others on all the internal doors, except those of the toilet and bathroom. Inside the case is a small scroll on which is handwritten the first two paragraphs of the Shema, the Jewish confession of faith, which begins 'Hear, O Israel: The Lord our God, the Lord is one' (Deuteronomy 6:4–9, 11, 13–21).

The presence of the mezuzah reminds the Jews, and others, that there is a home where the family keeps God's law and where love and friendship can be found. The practice of keeping the mezuzah on the doorpost accords with the biblical command, 'And you shall write them on the doorposts of your house and within your gates' (Deuteronomy 6:9).

On entering and leaving the home, a devout Jew will touch the mezuzah on the word Shaddai (Almighty), which is inscribed on the case or on a piece of scroll which is showing, and say, 'May the Almighty guard my going out and my coming in now and forever'.

A mezuzah.

■ TASKS

1. Make a mezuzah.

2. Write the words of the Shema on a scroll.

Menorah

The Jewish home will usually have a nine-branched candlestick called a *menorah* which is used at the festival of Chanukah (pronounced *hanukkah*). A candle is lit each night for the eight nights of the festival from the 'servant' candle in the middle. The family will also have two single candlesticks, probably in silver, which are lit at the Sabbath meal and on other special occasions. There may also be examples of Jewish art or a star of David, a Seder plate (for use at the Passover meal), a Kiddush cup and a spice box.

A menorah.

Food laws

Keeping a kosher kitchen *(kashrut)* is one of the major duties of the Jewish housewife. The Orthodox Jewish family will make sure that the food laws are carefully kept, but some of the families of the Reform strand of Judaism may not observe them strictly. The laws regarding food are from the Bible and mainly concern two things: forbidden foods and not eating meat in the same meal as milk. Anything which may be eaten is called *kosher* and anything that is not allowed is called *treife*.

There are restrictions on the eating of meat, fowl and fish. Meat must be from a herbivorous animal which has a cloven hoof and which chews the cud, i.e. beef and lamb. Pork is not allowed. Fowl may include turkey, chicken, duck and goose, but no birds of prey. The meat must be bought from a kosher butcher to ensure that the animal has been slaughtered painlessly by a Jewish man well versed in the Torah (Laws) and trained in this art. The meat has to be 'koshered' before it is cooked, which means it must be soaked in water for half an hour, then left, with salt sprinkled on it, to drain off blood. After a final rinse, the meat is ready for cooking.

Fish does not need any special preparations, but Jews must only eat fish which have fins and scales; rock salmon and shellfish are treife.

Dairy products such as milk and butter come from kosher animals; kosher cheese is not made from rennet of animals. Because margarine and oil may contain small quantities of treife animal fat, they too must be bought from a kosher shop. Jews must be careful over all foods containing dairy products, for example, cakes, biscuits and ice-creams. Gelatine is of animal origin and so makes some bought confectionery treife.

The rules about keeping meat and milk separate are based on the law, 'Thou shalt not seethe a kid in its mother's milk' (Exodus 23:19). Jews do not prepare, cook or eat milk products with meat products. They may not eat a milk pudding after a meat course and coffee with milk cannot be consumed until three hours after a meal containing meat. This practice has repercussions in the storing and preparation of food: meat and milk must be kept in separate cupboards or at least on separate shelves, and there must be two sets of cooking utensils, worktops, washing-up bowls and cloths. Meat products in fact take up very little space and everything else is classed as milk. To avoid the necessity of having two lots of worktops and two sinks, many Jews use a special board for preparing the meat and a washing-up bowl for the meat utensils. To avoid confusion, kitchen equipment is colour-coded, traditionally red for meat and blue for milk, although any colours can be used to tone in with the decor of the kitchen.

Food that can be eaten with both meat and milk is called *parve* and includes chicken, fish, fruit, vegetables and anything of pure vegetable origin.

■ TASKS

1. Play a game to help, particularly the young children, to remember which food is allowed and which foods can and cannot be eaten together. There are many forms the game could take. First, using small squares of cardboard, write the name of a food on each one including non-kosher foods. It would be fun, and easier for infants, if there were a picture of the food as well, cut out from a magazine perhaps. The children could then be asked to sort the foods into kosher and non-kosher.

Using all the kosher foods, ask the children to make them into meals that can be eaten by Jewish people. They will have to make sure that no meat products are put with milk products.

2. Plan menus. The children could imagine that they are having a Jewish friend to stay and that they have to plan a meal. The menus could be written neatly on card and illustrated. The finished work could be displayed.

3. Kosher grocer's shop. In the infant classroom, a shop corner stocking only kosher foods could be made. If there is a Jewish community close by, it will be easy to obtain packets. Sainsbury's stock Rakusen's matzohs – a type of crackerbread made without leaven, which is eaten all year round, but especially at Pesach (Passover).

4. Make 'Rules of the kitchen' posters. The really adventurous could embroider or screen-print them on tea towels or kitchen aprons.

5. Cook a Jewish dish, or a whole meal, and eat it (see recipes given on pp. 88-9, 121).

6. Older children could imagine they are starting up a Jewish home and need to plan and buy for their kosher kitchen.

Shabbat (Sabbath)

A Jewish day runs from evening to evening, so Shabbat begins at sunset on Friday and ends at nightfall on Saturday. Its observance is based on the fourth commandment: 'Remember the Sabbath Day to keep it holy'. There is no travel or work during the Sabbath, and this includes cooking, shopping, homework and even, in strictly Orthodox homes, turning lights on and off. Lights that may be needed are left on and all meals are cold. The special sabbath meal has to be prepared on Friday afternoon and the family must be home from school and work by sunset. In the winter months this will be quite early, which is why Jewish schools sometimes differ from others in their closing time on Fridays.

At home the mother lights two candles placed in the candlesticks on the table and says a blessing over them:

'You are our light, O Lord, and our Salvation. In your name we kindle these Sabbath lights. May they bring into our household the beauty of truth and the radiance of love's understanding. On this Sabbath eve, and at all times, Let there be light.'

After this the family, dressed in their best clothes, eat the best meal of the week. It begins with the father of the house saying Kiddush – a prayer ending with a blessing – over a goblet of wine, from which everyone takes a sip. Then, after a ritual washing of the hands, he removes the embroidered cover from the plaited loaves of bread, called *Challa* (pronounced halla) and says a blessing over it. Everyone eats a piece with a little salt on it – salt being a symbol of life and happiness – and then settles down to the meal. There are usually two loaves of bread to symbolise the double portion of manna left for the children of Israel in the wilderness on the Sabbath eve (see Exodus 16:22–35.)

There are synagogue services on Friday night and Saturday morning and an evening ceremony in the home as Sabbath ends. A Havdalah prayer is said and a plaited Havdalah candle lit. Havdalah means separation: this ceremony marks the separation between the holiness of the Sabbath and the working week. There are spices in a special box to remind people of the sweetness of the Sabbath. The father says a blessing over a lighted candle and some wine and spices, and the family prays silently for a week that will be as sweet as the aroma given off by the spices.

Hospitality is enjoined upon Jews by their religion and particularly on the Sabbath a Jewish family will invite a poor or lonely person into their home. A biblical precedent for this is the story of Abraham's hospitality to Lot and of his hospitality to three men who turned out to be angels.

Men and boy at prayer in a Synagogue.

Dress

The male Jew wears a skull cap, otherwise known as a *kipa* or *yarmulka*, as a sign of respect to God. All men and boys wear a *kipa* (pronounced keeper) in the synagogue (if you visit a synagogue, all the boys must wear one) and some wear them most of the time. The men also wear a *tallith* (prayer shawl) when praying in the synagogue or at home. They also wear *tefillin* (boxes containing scrolls of the scripture) on their head and arms if they are worshipping anywhere other than the synagogue.

Growing up in the faith

Apart from going to ordinary schools, the Jewish child will attend classes run by the synagogue, usually on a Sunday and sometimes on a weekday evening as well, at which they learn from the rabbi, or another senior Jew, about Jewish history, the Law, the scriptures and how to read and write Hebrew. This learning and understanding of the Jewish tradition culminates in the Bar Mitzvah (Son of the Law) or Bat Mitzvah ceremony at about age 13 when the boy or girl becomes an adult Jew and accepts responsibility for their own religious life.

In the synagogue the Torah is kept in the form of a scroll like the one below. It is written in Hebrew.

This is how the word 'Israel' is written in Hebrew.

■ TASK

Write the word Israel in Hebrew.

Islam

Great emphasis is placed upon the importance of the family in Islam and the Qur'an is most explicit about sexual morality, advocating fidelity and pre-marital chastity.

The home is important as a place of learning for the children and observance of the everyday rules of the religion. As in Judaism, the mother is central to the running of the home and keeping the religious practices. It is often asserted that the role of women in Islam is restrictive, but women are not barred from taking jobs outside the home as long as they still fulfil their duties within it. Muhammad urged men to treat women with respect and kindness and one of his sayings is 'Paradise is to be found at the feet of your mother' (see the story 'Your Mother! Your Mother! Your Mother!' on pp. 41-2). Once the sanctity of the family is recognised, it is easier to understand that the status of women in Islam is higher than Westerners would think at first sight.

Although polygamy is acceptable in Islam, it is more often the exception than the rule and economically it is often prohibitive. In some landowning societies, arranged marriages are common, in which the wealth and status of the families plays an important part. Usually marriages are arranged by the parents, who would try to suit their respective children's personalities, but the betrothed have the final say for a marriage is not valid without the consent of both partners.

Worship in the home

Full details are given on Muslim prayer in the next chapter, but here it may be noted that the Muslim is duty-bound to pray to Allah five times a day, wherever he or she is, including the home. The women do not usually attend the mosque for Friday worship and, where they are allowed, they must be kept out of the sight of the men so as not to distract them. More usually, the women will pray at home with the children and read to them from the Qur'an as part of their religious instruction.

Food laws

Muslims must also follow certain food laws: as with the Jews, the meat of the pig is forbidden to them, as are any foods which contain animal fat, for example, biscuits or ice cream. The eating of rodents, reptiles and carnivorous animals is also forbidden. Animals that Muslims eat must have been slaughtered in the correct fashion: the meat that is ritually killed according to Muslim practice is called *halal*, God's name being invoked as a sign of recognition that the life is being taken so that man might be fed and kept alive. Meat from kosher butchers is also acceptable.

To Muslims, alcohol, even used in cooking or for medical purposes, is forbidden because drinking it might lead to addiction and inability to serve one's family and the community properly. In addition the effects of alcohol render a person less able to communicate with God through prayer. A Muslim shopkeeper should not even sell alcohol to non-Muslims.

RECIPES

Tomato pilav   (SERVES 4)
2 medium tomatoes, skinned and chopped
2 oz/50 g butter
1 teaspoon ground coriander
pepper
½ teaspoon salt
1 tablespoon oil
1 onion, finely grated
¾ pint/375 ml beef stock
1 teaspoon tomato purée
7 oz/175 g long-grain rice
2 oz/50 g butter, melted

METHOD
Place the tomatoes, butter, salt, pepper and coriander in a saucepan. Cook over a medium heat for 5 mins until the mixture is thick. In a separate pan, heat the oil and fry the onion until soft, remove from the pan. Add the stock and tomato purée, bring to the boil and cook for 5 mins. Purée the mixture with the onion in a food processor. Measure the purée, top up with stock to make ¾ pint, bring to the boil on a high heat and pour on the rice. Reduce to a low heat, cover and simmer for 20 mins until all the liquid is absorbed. Add the melted butter and toss the rice until the grains are well coated. Cover the rice with a towel and leave to stand for 20 mins before serving.

Dolmas (SERVES 6)
5 tablespoons olive oil
4 oz/100 g onion, finely chopped
2 oz/50 g long-grain rice
grated rind of 2 lemons
1½ teaspoons ground coriander
1½ teaspoons ground cumin
pinch salt
freshly ground black pepper
4 oz/100 g minced lamb
1 oz/25 g pine kernels
1 oz/25 g currants
8 oz/200 g pack vine leaves

METHOD

Heat 2½ tablespoons oil in a heavy pan. Add the onion and cook for 5 mins. Add the rice, stirring for 3 mins until all the grains are coated in oil. Pour in ¼ pint/125 ml water, add the rind, spices and seasoning, bring to the boil. Reduce heat and simmer for 15 mins or until all liquid is absorbed. Heat 1 tablespoon oil in another pan, add the minced lamb, fry for 5 mins. Add pine kernels and fry for 5 mins. Remove mixture from pan and add to rice. Stir in the currants. Bring ¾ pint/375 ml water to the boil in a pan. Drop in the vine leaves and turn the heat off immediately. Soak the leaves for 1 min in the water, drain and plunge into a bowl of cold water to cool. Separate the leaves and place them, dull side uppermost, on kitchen paper to drain. Layer the bottom of a casserole with enough leaves to cover. Stuff remaining leaves with 1 tablespoon each of the rice mixture by placing the mixture in the centre of the leaf, turning up the stalk end and folding in the sides to enclose the stuffing. Starting at the stalk end, roll the leaves tightly into a cigar shape. Place the leaves, seam side down, in the casserole, sprinkle with the remaining oil and 1–2 tablespoons water. Cover with a lid. Place casserole over a high heat for approximately 3 mins, reduce heat and simmer for a further 50 mins. Remove lid, cool before serving.

Dress

Tunic and pants or saris are worn by the women and, to observe rules of modesty, they must cover their arms and legs as well as their bodies. Muslim girls in school wear long trousers for P.E. In hot countries men also wear tunic and pants, and also lozenge-shaped hats, but in this country many adopt Western styles of dress.

A Muslim girl wearing the traditional shalwar and kameez.

■ TASKS

1. Dress up in tunic and pants or a sari. (Instructions for wrapping a sari are given on p. 48.)

2. Dress dolls in saris.

3. Wrap a sari on a tailor's dummy.

4. Make up the recipes.

Growing up in Islam

When a Muslim child is born calls of worship are spoken into both its ears, including the phrase, 'Prayer is better than sleep'. The baby's head is completely shaved, the hair weighed and the same weight in gold given to the poor. Boys are circumcised at an early age.

Until children are old enough to be taught in the mosque they are taught from the Qur'an at home by their mother. This starts at the age of four, and is marked by a family feast. The first thing they learn is the *Kalimah:*

'There is only one God and Muhammad is the last of the prophets.'

They learn Arabic so they can recite the Qur'an in the exact words that God gave to Muhammad. They must also learn to treat the holy book with proper respect. Before reading from the Qur'an, a devout Muslim will remove the special cover from the book, kiss it and place it on a special stand.

Boys learn Arabic and the teachings and history of Islam from the *imam* (the Muslim prayer leader and teacher of religion), who holds classes in the mosque every evening. When a child is able to recite the Qur'an from memory, he or she is given the title 'Hafiz', meaning memoriser, and is held in great respect. Boys and girls are taught separately and the girls are always taught by a woman, either at home or in class.

A Muslim and his Qur'an stand.

■ **TASK**

Make a Qur'an stand.

    a. Take two pieces of thick card 19 × 29 cm.

    b. 15 cm from the top of each piece of card, make a cut 11 cm long.

    c. Slot the two pieces of card together to form a stand.

    d. Decorate the stand with geometric patterns. (You could cut the patterns out, paint them, or make them with pieces of coloured and foil paper.)

Your mother! Your mother! Your mother!

ONE DAY, a man came to see the Prophet (Peace and Blessings be upon him).* It seemed clear that he was puzzling over some problem. People used to come to the Blessed Prophet with all sorts of problems, but not with those they could solve for themselves. So this one must have been very important to him to bring him to the Blessed Prophet.

'Tell me, O prophet!' the man asked, 'I have many relatives and many friends whom I love and whom I wish to care for and help. But I often find it difficult to decide which of them has the greatest claim upon me? Which of them should come first?'

The Blessed Prophet replied immediately: 'Your mother should come first and before all others.'

The man was very pleased to have this clear guidance from the Blessed Prophet. But, of course, there were all his other relatives, and his friends to think of. So, he asked: 'And after my mother, who has the greatest claim upon me?'

The Blessed Prophet's reply this second time surprised him. 'Your mother!' the Blessed Prophet said again.

Have I heard right? The man wondered. Why was the Blessed Prophet repeating himself? Perhaps he had not spoken clearly, the man thought, or maybe the Blessed Prophet had not heard him properly. So, the man asked his question again: 'What I want to know is, after my mother, who has the greatest claim upon me?' Again, the Blessed Prophet uttered the same words: 'Your mother!'

Your mother, your mother, your mother: the Blessed Prophet had now said it three times. Slowly, the man realised why he had done so: 'The Blessed Prophet means that my mother is extremely important, so much so that my duty to her must be stressed over and over again. Even so', the man's thoughts ran on, 'what about all the others I love and wish to care for?'

41

Still uncertain and wanting to know more, the man turned once more to the Blessed Prophet. 'And after I have done my duty to my mother, who comes after her? Is there anyone beside her?'

The Blessed Prophet answered: 'After your mother, your father.'

'And then?' asked the man.

'Your nearest kinfolk', the Blessed Prophet told him.

Now, at last, his duties were clear to him. He was to serve his mother before anyone else, and then he was to care for his father, children, grandparents, brothers, sisters, uncles, aunts, until he had done his duty by all his relatives.

From *Love at Home,* Khurram Murad (Islamic Foundation, 1986)

* Muslims are required to invoke Allah's blessing and peace upon the prophet whenever his name is mentioned.

Hinduism

Social arrangements

Traditionally Hindu family groups living under one roof or close to each other are large – what the sociologists term 'extended families'. In such a set-up the head of the family, normally the oldest living man, lives with his wife, unmarried daughters, sons and their wives and children. His granddaughters eventually, if they marry, go to live with their husband's family; his grandsons will bring their wives to the home. The head of the family owns the land and the house and has ultimate authority over the others.

There are still traces of a different style of family organisation in India, which used to be common in the south, where the family consists of a woman and her children, her sisters and brothers and their sons and daughters. The husbands do not live in the house, but each visits his wife from time to time. The men do not have authority over their own children, but over their sisters' children.

In recent years economic changes in India have brought social changes and it is increasingly common for families to be nuclear, consisting only of parents and their children. In Britain Hindu families are very likely to be nuclear, although elderly relatives may live with the 'nucleus' for economic or health reasons.

The Hindu family may experience the tensions which are inevitable with extended families. But the advantages will also be there: the young can learn from the wisdom of the old, and the old can be cared for when they get frail. There is always someone to talk to and to share the work. Each person has family duties to perform as well as responsibilities of caste, school and work.

Hindu marriages are traditionally arranged by the parents of the couple concerned. Often the joining of two families and similar backgrounds and wealth motivates the match as much as consideration of caste. The ceremony will take place in the bride's community; once married she will go to live with her husband, and perhaps his family as well.

The Hindu mother's role will differ in Britain from the one she fulfils in the small rural villages of India. For instance, in Britain, she may go out to work to boost the family finances, in which case she has a very busy life for she must see to the family in the morning and complete the housework at night. There is a tradition of powerful women in Hindu societies – politicians, queens, poets, authors, philosophers and warriors – so in theory there is little resistance to Hindu women pursuing a career, and many do so in this country. Perhaps the existence of many goddesses as well as gods in Hinduism indicates the respect which a Hindu husband ideally shows for his wife. Traditionally a husband has no say in the running of the home and does little to help even if his wife has a paid job as well. The Hindu housewife is very much in control: she gives her husband an allowance from the family income, rather than him giving her the housekeeping money. As a mark of respect and esteem, the Hindu wife and mother is given the title Devi meaning goddess and Ji, a further mark of respect, may be added so that Deviji is an addition to her name.

The family shrine

Each home has a place set aside for the worship of the gods. This may be a whole room or an alcove, depending on the space available. There will be pictures or statues of one god or more, a table, and perhaps tinsel to brighten up the shrine. Every morning and evening, the family prays and offers worship (*puja*) at the shrine. This takes place after bathing and before eating to ensure cleanliness of mind and body when approaching God. Although they may use a bath, most Hindus prefer flowing water such as from a shower or, in India, a stream or river. At the puja ceremony lamps and incense are lit and a small bell rung as an offering of flowers or fruit is placed in front of the deity.

One of the prayers that is always offered in the morning is from the Gayatri Mantra and is addressed to the god of light:

*'Let us think on the lovely splendour of God, Savitr:
May he bring light into our minds!'*

In the evening, part of the meal is offered to the god the family particularly honours, a ritual known as *prasad* (pronounced prashard). It is believed that the god blesses the food, which is then received back and eaten.

Hinduism is not a congregational religion; within guidelines of traditional custom people can worship God as they choose. There are no classes instructing the young in their religion. It is up to the family to introduce their children to their particular strand of religion and to point them to the scriptures. This education, along with daily worship, takes place in the home. Special family events such as birth, marriage and death are marked at the family shrine.

■ TASKS

1. Make a family shrine. You could drape a sari or brightly coloured piece of fabric over a table and put statues and/or pictures of the gods on it and decorate with tinsel. Add a couple of small candles and some incense and you have a shrine. You can obtain the necessary objects from a Hindu centre or R.E. resources centre.

2. Write out the above prayer and decorate with typical Hindu patterns (see Chapter 4 for ideas).

3. Consider how the family shrine and puja twice a day would affect family life. Would you like to have a similar ceremony each day in your family or not? Give reasons.

Food

Traditionally, Hindus are vegetarian because they believe all animal life (including the tiniest insects) has a soul and do not like to kill such beings. The cow in particular is sacred, so beef is particularly prohibited. However, those living in Britain may adapt out of convenience to include some meat, poultry and fish in their diet, particularly the young who wish to eat in school and in the homes of friends. Nevertheless, the staple diet of the Hindu family is likely to be rice, vegetables and pulses, with meat on occasions.

Indian food is characterised by spices, which link the Hindu family in Britain to their homeland and indeed their whole culture. To complement and lessen the lingering taste of the hot spices such as chillis, Hindus eat very sweet desserts. These can be bought from Indian delicatessens. If you are not used to them, these can seem sickly but semolina puddings and natural yoghurts are also eaten and are more palatable to Westerners. Food is often eaten with the fingers or with the aid of a chappatti (a wheat pancake). (The emphasis on washing the body in Hinduism makes practical sense in this context!)

■ TASKS

1. Try cooking and eating a Hindu meal or sampling small tastes of a few dishes. The recipes below can be made up in the classroom, with the use of a Calor Gas stove. (See also other Indian recipes in Chapters 4 and 5.)

2. You could buy some Indian spices, pickles and sweets. If you do not feel like cooking and live near enough to an Indian delicatessen, perhaps at least let the children smell some of the spices: chilli, cumin, coriander, cardamom, turmeric, cayenne pepper, paprika, mustard seeds, ginger root. These can be bought in ordinary delicatessens and powdered versions of most of them are stocked in supermarkets. It is also easy to make barfi and Indian sweets (see opposite and p. 76).

RECIPES

Chicken with tomatoes and garam masala (Timatar Murghi)

Serves six and is good accompanied by plain long-grain rice.

5 tablespoons vegetable oil
¾ teaspoon whole cumin seeds
1 inch (2.5 cm) of cinnamon stick
6 whole cardamom pods
2 bay leaves
¼ teaspoon whole peppercorns
6 oz onion peeled and finely chopped
6–7 cloves garlic, peeled and finely chopped
1-inch (2.5-cm) cube fresh ginger, peeled and finely chopped
1 lb (450 g) tinned chopped tomatoes
1½ teaspoons salt
½ teaspoon garam masala
⅛–½ teaspoon cayenne pepper
3 lb (1.35 kg) chicken pieces

METHOD

Heat oil in large pot or wok over medium flame. When hot, add cumin seeds, cinnamon, cardamom, bay leaves and peppercorns. Stir once, then add garlic, onion and ginger. Stir until onion begins to brown. Add tomatoes, chicken, salt and cayenne pepper. Stir to mix and bring to the boil. Cover tightly, turn the heat to low and simmer for 25 mins or until the chicken is tender. Stir a few times to prevent sticking. Remove cover and turn heat to medium. Sprinkle on garam masala and stir over heat for about 5 mins. Remove the whole spices before eating.

Barfi

Box of Ostermilk no.2 baby milk
Small tin of evaporated milk
½ lb of sugar
½ pint of water
1 teaspoon of rosewater (from chemist) to taste
4 oz grated almonds

METHOD

In a large saucepan, mix the Ostermilk powder with evaporated milk. Mix the water and sugar in another pan and bring to the boil. Add rosewater and the milk mixture and stir well. Pour the mixture into a flan dish in a thin layer and sprinkle with almonds. After about 10 minutes, cut it into 2-inch cubes and it is ready to serve.

Clothes

Hindu women usually wear saris, although in Britain some may adopt Western styles of dress if their occupation demands it. A sari is a length of material of about six metres, which is draped around the body. Under the sari a woman may wear an ankle-length skirt in a fabric of contrasting colour into which the sari is tucked to secure it. Another form of dress is *shalwar* – trousers with elasticated ankles – worn under a tunic. A separate garment called a *dopatta* covers the head.

1 Tuck sari into waist petticoat, winding it round the left side.
2 Take material round waist once more, not tucking it in.
3 Put end of material round shoulders.

4 Take loose end and put over left shoulder.
5 Gather loose material in front into pleats.
6 Tuck pleats firmly into waist.

■ TASKS

1. Wrap a sari around someone in class or around a tailor's dummy.

2. Children could each bring a length of material and a doll and dress them in saris for a display.

3. Young children could have an Indian dressing-up corner for the duration of the topic.

4. Using as a basis the patterns on the fabric of a sari, work could be done on patterns, printing by potato, wood block or even screen. The children could design their own sari, print the fabric and dress a dummy in it. (Sometimes travel agents have life-size cardboard models of Indian women you could use.)

Growing up in the Hindu way

When a child is born, the family priest chants *mantras* (prayers) to ward off any evil spirits and bring the child the blessings of health and long life. On the twelfth day of life, the baby is placed in a swinging crib with twelve lamps burning beneath it. The priest pronounces the baby's name, which has been chosen by the parents, and the women sing songs into which are inserted the child's name at appropriate places. There is a feast at which gold or silver objects are given to the child and its ears are pierced and ornamented with a small hoop of thin gold wire. At four months the child has its first outing to see the light of day, at which time prayers are said in the temple. At one year boy babies have their first haircut, which symbolises cutting away any evil from a former life that the child might have brought to this one.

At the age of eight or older – when he is capable of learning the scriptures in their original Sanskrit – a boy undertakes the sacred thread ceremony. This is a big event, a religious ceremony and gift-giving after which the family will have a dinner party followed by light refreshments for other relatives and acquaintances. The ceremony is as follows. After bathing, the boy sits with his father and the priest by the sacred fire. The priest takes the sacred thread and places it over the boy's head so that it hangs from his left shoulder, across his chest and round beneath his right arm. Mantras are chanted and the priest then chants the Gayatri

Hymn from the Rig Veda, while the father whispers it into his son's right ear. The boy repeats the hymn. He is now considered old enough to start learning the Sanskrit scriptures.

From the *Gayatri Hymn*

Om bhuh, bhuvah, swaha,
Tat savituh varenyam bhargo
Devasya dhimahi. Dhiyo yo nah
Prachodayat.

(We contemplate the most radiant lustre of God *Savita* (the sun), the sustainer of Earth, Inter-Space and Heaven. May He inspire our intellect.)

From *Taittiriya Aryanaka (The Forest Book)*

Satyam vada. Dharmam chara.
Swadhyan maa pramadah.
Matradevo bhava.
Pitradevo bhava.
Archaryadevo bhava.
Rashtradevo bhava.

(Speak the truth. Follow your Dharma (moral duty). Never neglect your studies. Honour your mother, father, teacher and nation.)

■ TASKS (Level One)

1. Calligraphy. Write out Sanskrit hymn extract and decorate it.

2. Discuss (and write about) initiation ceremonies within the children's experience. Some may have witnessed infant baptism (christening) or confirmation. Others may have been enrolled as Cubs or Brownies and have had to make promises and do certain things to qualify.

3 WORSHIP AND BUILDINGS

Central to any religion is the worship of God and the building in which this takes place. The architecture of religious buildings is normally distinctive, but the circumstances of the devotees influence this. Thus Muslims and Hindus living as a minority group in other countries, such as Britain, may not be wealthy enough to build a distinctive place of worship but may have to adapt an existing building to their needs, for example, buying a house and transforming the inside. Some Hindu communities have been known to rent the local church hall on the days they need it.

The best way to bring forms of worship alive is through experience. That is not to say that the children should be made to take part in rituals that are alien to their own culture. They may consider, if they are mature enough, whether these methods of worship might be helpful and what they like about them without actually taking part. A lot of visual and aural stimulus is valuable here. There is a list of addresses to write to for tapes, slides and posters on pp. 124–5.

Probably the way to make a lasting impression upon the pupils is to visit places of worship. R.E. resource centres may be able to put you in touch with religious leaders who will welcome you in their sacred buildings. Make sure that you find out at the planning stages if there are any customs you must observe to save embarrassment or offence when you get there. When visiting a synagogue, the boys will have to wear a skull cap or equivalent. Some synagogues provide these – others may not, but will allow visiting boys in with any headgear. Girls will probably have to cover arms and legs and heads when visiting a mosque.

The worship and buildings of Judaism, Islam and Hinduism are dealt with singly in this chapter, but you may want to adapt the approach to a comparative study. Alternatively, you may want to use the section on Judaism in tandem with the information about Jewish family life in the previous chapter and devote a project to Judaism generally. The information given here on places of worship may also suit a project on the local environment, if your area includes people of these faiths.

There are suggested tasks at the end of each section. A general task relevant to all sections is learning the vocabulary associated with places and forms of worship. One way of making it easier is to play simple games that continually place the words in context. One possibility is to make small jigsaws. The simplest jigsaw would be in sets of two pieces, e.g. 'A Jew worships in a' on one card would match up with 'synagogue' on another card, perhaps accompanied by a picture. A four-piece jigsaw might have 'Hindu' on one piece, 'temple' on another, 'Hinduism' on the third and the name of a god on the fourth. There are many possible variations. (See p.103 for an illustration of a jigsaw relating to Islam.)

Judaism

The synagogue

The special building in which Jews worship is called a synagogue. The word synagogue is of Greek origin and means 'a gathering' or meeting place. This is as appropriate today as it ever was for the synagogue exists not only for worship, but also for meetings, study and celebrations. There is more to a synagogue than the area for worship. This might be on the ground floor while the basement houses the classrooms and functions hall.

Some synagogues in Britain are purpose-built; others are converted older buildings. There is no particular architectural style – some may be ornate and others very simple – but they can often be recognised by a star of David on the outside wall. Where there are strong and prosperous Jewish communities, for example in London, Leeds, Liverpool and Manchester, there are several purpose-built synagogues. In areas where there are only a few Jewish families, a small building may be rented or bought, which is what happened in Chester until circumstances forced the congregation to travel to Liverpool for services. A synagogue, whether temporary or permanent, can be wherever the ark is, just as it was for the ancient Jews as they wandered during the period of the Judges.

A synagogue in Britain.

The ark is a box or cupboard which contains the scrolls of the Law (Torah). The scrolls are handwritten on parchment and are extremely valuable, not only for their religious content but also because they can each take a year for a scribe to complete and so are expensive to purchase. Each scroll is protected with an embroidered cover and some also have a little silver breastplate and an ornament with bells on mounted on the wooden poles of the scroll. The ornament is called a crown to accord with the majesty of the Law. When the cover is put on the scroll this is called 'dressing the scroll'. Above the ark is a lamp which is always lit to symbolise the eternal presence of God. In the past this would have been an oil lamp, but these days it is an electric light bulb, sometimes with its own generator so that it is not affected by power cuts.

In the centre of the synagogue or at the front is the *bimah* (platform) from which the service is conducted. When it is time for a reading from the scroll, it is taken from the ark, uncovered and placed upon a table or lectern. The reader uses a silver pointer called a *yad*, to help guide his eye along the script. This is like a stick with a small hand on the end, its index finger pointing at the scroll, and is used in order to reduce handling of the scroll. In a Reform synagogue, all the family can sit together, but in an Orthodox synagogue the women sit behind a screen or on a balcony. The women have authority and religious duties to carry

53

out in the home, as well as responsibility for the children, and so are not expected to attend the synagogue, although they are very welcome if they do.

Worship

The main synagogue services take place on Friday evening and Saturday morning as part of the Sabbath (see also pp. 33–4). Orthodox synagogues will also have a Saturday evening service. At other times of the year there are special services to mark the festivals, as well as Bar Mitzvahs, weddings and funerals.

Services in Orthodox synagogues are conducted in Hebrew and led by the *cantor* (singer), whereas the Reform Jews worship in a mixture of Hebrew and the vernacular. Jewish worship does not have to be led by a rabbi. It can be led by an adult Jew who is fluent enough in Hebrew and can chant correctly from the scrolls and for the prayers. The rabbi does not even have to be present. Rabbis are not priests. The word means 'teacher': the rabbi's job is to study and explain the Jewish Law to the people.

In the services, the rabbi and all the male members of the congregation wear a fringed prayer shawl made of wool or silk, called a *tallith*, the tassels of which remind them never to forget God's Law. They also wear skull caps as a sign of respect to God. There is a reading from the Torah, the whole of which is read during the year. The rabbi may then explain the meaning of the passage or he may give a sermon applying Jewish principles to topical events or matters of morality. There are also prayers, some ancient and traditional and some new, which relate to topical world events and concerns of the congregation. Jews never kneel to pray – they either sit or stand.

■ TASKS

1. Build two models showing respectively the outside and inside of a synagogue.

2. Make a stained-glass window showing a star of David. This can be done using coloured tissue paper inset into black sugar paper.

3. A more advanced activity would be to make stained-glass scenes from Old Testament stories, such as Noah's Ark or Joseph and his dreams. In this case, the stories could be read and acted. There is music to go with each of the above-mentioned, which the children could learn in music sessions or at least listen to: *Joseph and the Amazing Technicolour Dreamcoat* by Tim Rice and Andrew Lloyd Webber (Novello, 1968); and *Captain Noah and his Floating Zoo* by Michael Flanders and Joseph Horovitz (Novello, 1973). Bear in mind that Orthodox Jews do not allow such representations in the stained glass of their synagogue windows: 'Thou shalt not make for thyself a graven image . . .'.

4. Make a scroll from white sugar paper, ironed to give it an older look. Write the script carefully in black ink, for example, the first of the Ten Commandments from Exodus 20. The two sides may be attached to wooden poles, e.g., drumsticks or pieces of cane. Perhaps various members of the class could each contribute a page which could all be stuck together, reading from right to left as in Hebrew (see the illustration on p. 35).

Since Torah scrolls are very precious and we do not wish to imply that they mean no more than a piece of sugar paper and a bit of bamboo, we must encourage the children to treat them with respect and keep them in a special box. Some pupils could make a cover for the scroll.

5. Make a scroll cover, most suitably from blue velvet, if any can be obtained. Blue is a favoured colour. A Star of David could be embroidered on the front, perhaps in silver thread, along with fancy borders as time and imagination allow.

Islam

Muslims worship in a mosque on a Friday, their holy day, and at times of special festivals. The word 'mosque' means 'place of prostration': Muslims adopt a position of total prostration when they pray. Praying takes place on individual prayer mats; there are no chairs or pews in a mosque. In each mosque is an archway *(mihrab)*, positioned so that in turning towards it worshippers are facing Mecca, as their custom requires.

Although many mosques are very ornate – typically with domes and a tower called a minaret – they can be very simple, particularly in

Mosque of Omar, or Dome of the Rock, in Jerusalem.

Britain where the Muslim community may have to use an ordinary house, adapted to meet their needs. Characteristic of Islamic architecture are the geometric shapes, often in blue and gold, as for example in the Dome of the Rock, Jerusalem, or the mosque at Medina.

■ TASKS

1. A simple class activity is to make a frieze showing mosques against a sunset. Some children can cut out mosque shapes in black sugar paper, perhaps using a cardboard template, while others colour-wash white paper depicting the setting of the sun. Geometric shapes, drawn on strips of white paper, can be added for effect.

2. A more advanced activity would be to design and build a model mosque. Coloured tin foil and sweet papers are useful for decoration.

3. Typical colours in Islamic art are blue and gold and, as we have seen, geometric shapes are popular. A colour theme of blue and gold could be used in art and craft work. Strips of black sugar paper look effective with blue and gold shapes stuck on them. The children could arrange the shapes in particular sequences as part of maths activities, and the strips could then form a border on the display areas.

To extend these themes further, there could be a colour table to which children could bring items. Further work could be done on shapes depending on the age of the children. Infants may find it rewarding to make pictures using shapes, e.g. houses and people. They could experiment with 3-D octagons and wooden shapes to make patterns. Older children could make more complicated patterns using these shapes and begin to learn about the properties of various shapes.

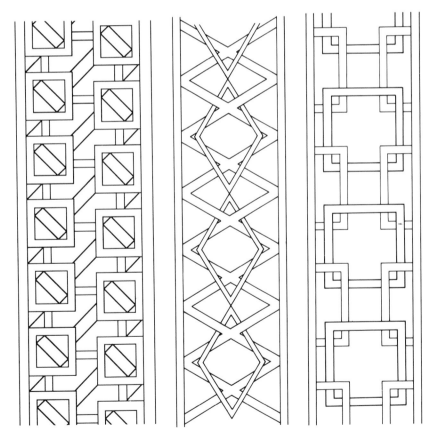

Geometric patterns such as these are typical of the ones found in mosques.

57

4. There is a great fascination with numbers in Islam. Times of prayer and the inheritance of property have always been calculated through the use of quadratic equations. The mathematicians became interested in the 'magic number squares' where the numbers add up to the same whether added diagonally, horizontally or vertically, as in this example.

8	1	6
3	5	7
4	9	2

For further ideas on how to use Islamic mathematical ideas see the article by Ray Hemmings in *Multi-Racial Education* (Summer, 1980). There is also a useful *Islamic Colouring Book* by David Wade (Wildwood House, 1976).

Prayer

A Muslim string of prayer beads.

When a Muslim worships, he declares his belief in 'one God' with Muhammad as his prophet. The mention of Muhammad's name is always accompanied by the phrase 'praises and blessings be upon Him', sometimes abbreviated to p.b.u.h. when written. Muslims are not allowed to make any image of God or of human beings, but some use a string of prayer beads, called *subha*, usually 99 in number to represent the 99 excellent names of God.

Muslims pray facing Mecca, the birthplace of Muhammad. First worshippers wash themselves thoroughly *(wadhu)* in strict order – hands, mouth, nostrils, face, arms, head, ears, neck and feet – so that they may be rid of any impurities and be symbolically spiritually clean. Mosques have a special room for these ablutions. Prayers are said standing and kneeling on a prayer mat. There are special positions for prayer, starting upright and including complete prostration. There is no singing in the mosque so that there can be no human interpretation of the words of Allah. The day for praying in the mosque is Friday, but it is usually only the men and older boys who attend while the women and girls pray at home. It is the woman's job to teach the children how to pray.

Muslims must pray five times a day wherever they are – at home or at work. The times will vary according to the time of the year, but they are approximately: between dawn and sunrise; between noon and mid-afternoon; between mid-afternoon and sunset; between sunset and darkness and before going to sleep.

The *muezzin* calls Muslims to prayer from the minaret of the mosque beginning with the words 'Allahu Akbar' (Allah, the greatest...). Those who do not live near a mosque have to rely on knowing the times of prayer. Sometimes employers do not mind the few minutes during the day that their Muslim employees must spend at prayer. Some Muslims clock off for the duration of their prayers and on again when they have finished so they are not paid for that time. If they are travelling at the time for prayer, they usually wait until they reach their destination.

■ TASKS

1. Make a class prayer mat approximately 61 × 91 cm (2 × 3 ft) using latticed fabric. Simple geometric patterns can be embroidered and felt shapes (in blue and gold) stuck on with glue. If each child works on a small piece, all these can be joined together at the end of the project to form a class prayer mat.

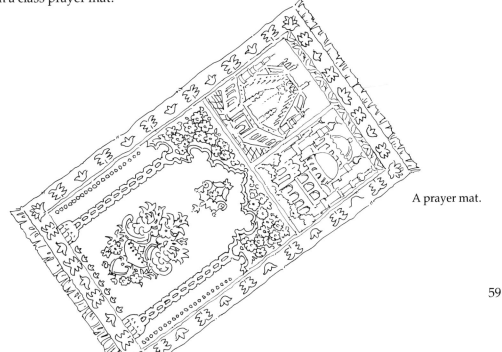

A prayer mat.

2. Another way to make a prayer mat is to use an old piece of material or sacking of the same size. Using coloured wool, sew a fringe to the two widths. Cut out from felt and/or other fabrics a basic mosque or *mihrab* for the front part of the prayer mat, and flowers or patterns for the part on which the worshipper stands. Cut out geometric shapes to border the edges of the mat. Glue the pieces to the mat.

Older children may be capable of embroidering the mat or sewing the fabric shapes to the backcloth. This is an activity that can be adapted to the children's skills and fit in with any other craft work that has been going on in the school.

3. Drawings can be done of the different prayer positions. Alternatively, cut-outs in black of the positions could be placed on a coloured background for an effective display.

These are the positions a Muslim should use when he prays.

Note: It is worth reminding the children that no representations of God or Muhammad are allowed in Islamic art.

Hinduism

Temples

Hindu worship takes place in the home at the family shrine, in Indian villages at outdoor shrines and in the temples. Hinduism is not a congregational religion; most worship is individual. Congregational hymn singing is popular, however, and in immigrant communities, Hindus may meet for worship partly as an attempt to maintain their corporate identity.

Courtyard of the
Birla Temple,
Delhi.

In England there are few Hindu temples; occasional gatherings for worship often take place in a hired hall. In some places there is a Hindu centre rather than an actual temple. A temple is regarded primarily as the home of the deity to whom it is dedicated. At least one priest is attached to each one to look after the god and supervise rituals. In India there are two main styles of temple, the Indo-Aryan in the north and Dravidian in the south. In shape the Indo-Aryan ones are based on a polygon with the inner sanctum in the centre directly beneath the main tower, which is characterised by curvilinear towers with rounded tops. The Dravidian temples look rather like rectangular pyramids, appearing almost to rise naturally from the terrain. They are bounded by high walls and large gateways. Carved into the stone of the temples are many images of the gods and scenes from the legends concerning them.

Inside the temples there are no seats, just large open areas resembling paved courtyards. Just outside the walls will be an oblong man-made lake in which the worshippers will bathe to ensure that they are ritually clean before entering the temple. The shrine in the centre of the temple houses the image of the deity, decorated with jewels and surrounded by the fresh flowers offered by devotees. In front of the shrine is an entrance hall in which to meditate before entering singly for worship. There may be small shrines all around the temple dedicated to

61

other gods and areas where gurus (religious teachers) sit to study and discuss the religious writings with their students.

Worship

Temple priests spend most of the day in worship. First of all, the image of the temple's god (who always symbolises the God, or Brahman) is awakened and greeted as you would an honoured guest in your house. Then he or she is washed, dressed and offered food so as to be ready to receive worshippers. The food, after being symbolically consumed by the image, is offered to worshippers as sacred food – *prasad*. Music is played to bring joy to the image and he or she is then ready to receive worshippers. The devotees may watch the priests perform these acts and will come forward and make their offerings to God, light a lamp and say their prayers. In the evening, the priest washes the image and retires it to bed. This caring for the image represents the devotion and love the faithful feel for God.

Temple interior, images in Gauri Shankar Temple.

Hindu worship is very individual. It does not have to take place in a temple, but can be performed in the home and can alternatively consist of yoga and meditation. Many Hindus, however, like to visit the most sacred shrines dedicated to the god they particularly honour.

Pilgrimage

Apart from trying to visit the important temples dedicated to the god he particularly worships, each Hindu tries to get to Benares to bathe in the river Ganges there at least once in a lifetime. The Ganges is the holiest river to Hindus and they believe that by bathing in it at Benares they will release their souls from *samsara* (the cycle of life and death). While in Benares, the pilgrims worship at the temple dedicated to Shiva and some of them take home some water from the Ganges in a sealed copper vessel. This may be used in the future when the need arises, perhaps to anoint a dying relative.

Worship in Hindu centres in Britain

Although Hindu worship is largely a personal thing, in Great Britain the Hindus may have no temple nearby and at specific times may hire a hall, perhaps one attached to a church. This provides a good excuse to meet with one another as well as an occasion for worshipping God.

At a meeting of this kind incense will be burning and the devout will sing their Hindu hymns to the accompaniment of a *sitar* and chant their prayers. The Hindu scriptures will be read and there may be a solo song and music from one of the Indian instruments. Sometimes there may be a visiting speaker – perhaps someone of distinction from India – but the services are usually informal. The food that the worshippers offer to God at the service, *prasad* is shared out and eaten and there may be a big meal for all the congregation.

At all services the ceremony of *arti* is carried out. A dish containing small candles or a small fire is held before each shrine. Fire, often used in Hindu rituals, is symbolic of the enrichment and enlightment given by God. After this, each individual may take the blessings of *arti* by holding their hands above the flames and then putting their hands over their face.

■ TASKS

1. Find out about Indian instruments and how they work. Use the book *Guru Nanak and the Snake* by Ruth Parmiter and Monica Price (Cassell, 1989) to learn some Indian inspired songs and stories.

2. Listen to Hindu music. Try movement to it. Consider how it differs from Western music.

3. Build a shrine (see p. 45 for ideas) and place incense, tinsel and flowers on it. Play some Indian music and imagine how it would feel to worship God in that atmosphere. Would it help you or not?

4 DIWALI

Background

Diwali (pronounced, and sometimes spelt, Divali) is one of the happiest of many Hindu festivals. Some Hindu festivals are connected with the seasons or with local legendary events and are not celebrated universally, but Diwali has a wide appeal, although there are variations in the form of its celebration, according to different beliefs and practices with Hinduism.

The festival occurs at the end of October and lasts for three or five days: the first two being the last two days of the Hindu month Asvina and the concluding day(s) the first (three) of Karttika. The traditional Diwali lights contrast starkly against the moonless sky at the end of Asvina, but a new moon appears at the beginning of Karttika. In parts of northern India, this time is regarded as the start of the new year.

Various Hindu stories are remembered at Diwali, concerned mainly with the god Vishnu and his wife Lakshmi, and their incarnation in human form to defeat evil on earth. One of the most popular stories is the following, which appears in the great Hindu epic, the Ramayana. It concerns Rama and Sita.

The triumph of Rama and Sita

KING DASHARATHA was a wise and powerful King who lived with his family in Ayodhya. He promised two wishes to one of his three wives, Queen Kaikeyi. She was jealous of the King's eldest son, Rama (an incarnation of the god Vishnu), and used one of her wishes to force him to appoint her son Bharata as successor to the throne. To make sure that Rama was out of the way, the Queen had him banished from Ayodhya for fourteen years.

Rama, his wife Sita and his brother Lakshmana faced many tribulations during their exile in the forest. The most difficult one was when the ten-headed demon king Ravana tricked the two men into leaving Sita alone, then abducted her and took her away to his kingdom on the island of Lanka.

Rama and Lakshmana searched in vain for Sita and eventually, in despair, called upon Durga, the goddess of motherhood, for help. Hanuman, the monkey warrior, showed Rama that Sita was being held by Ravana in Lanka. With the help of an army of animals, they built a bridge across the sea from India to Lanka. Even a little squirrel helped by rolling in the dust then shaking it to fill the cracks between the stones in the bridge. The other animals laughed at his attempts, but Rama gently stroked the squirrel to show his gratitude. From that day on it was said that squirrels in India had three yellow bands across their backs to show the caress of Rama's fingers.

After five days the bridge was completed and Rama and Lakshmana were able to cross over to Lanka, where, aided by Hanuman and his band of monkeys, they fought a terrible battle. Rama and Ravana fought a deadly duel, the outcome of which was for a long time uncertain until, using a magic bow given to him by Durga, Rama pierced Ravana's massive chest with an arrow fashioned from sun and fire and the demon king fell down dead.

This might seem like the end of the story, but Rama began to wonder whether Sita had been faithful to him during their enforced separation. The innocent Sita was so distressed by Rama's doubts that she wanted to die. She made a funeral fire and walked into the scorching flames. Agni, the god of fire, protected her and when Rama saw her emerge unharmed from the fire, he knew that she had been true to him all along and that her love had never died.

Finally, amidst great happiness, Rama and Sita returned to Ayodhya at the end of their fourteen years of exile. Their arrival was greeted with great rejoicing – even Rama's stepmother was pleased to see them. She had by then repented of her wrong-doing. Her son, Bharata, who had since become King, was also delighted for he had never felt that it was right for him to rule the country in Rama's stead. Throughout the years he had kept a pair of Rama's sandals on the throne to show who was the true King.

In celebration, the people of Ayodhya danced and put lighted lamps in their windows to illuminate the way home for Rama and Sita. The lights celebrated bravery and goodness and the triumph of love and truth over evil. It seemed, with the return of the real King and Queen, that the kingdom of Ayodhya had a new beginning and some say that the goddess Lakshmi came at this time bringing peace and prosperity.

How Diwali is celebrated

There are two main aspects to remember in the celebrating of Diwali. The feeling that there is a new start, and the celebration of the triumph of good over evil. The festival falls just after the monsoon season and marks the start of the dry season, when new seeds are planted ready for next year's harvest. To get rid of the musty smell of the monsoon air, and to attract Lakshmi the goddess of prosperity who is said to avoid dirty, dark houses, mustard oil is burnt in clay *diwa* lamps and homes given a good clean and perhaps some re-decoration. Some families devote a corner of their house to Lakshmi. This small shrine may contain a picture or statue of her surrounded by fruit and flowers, lights and candles. A *puja* (prayer) tray may be set at the shrine on which there are brightly coloured garlands in the sacred colours of red and orange, and various symbolic objects: rice to attract a good harvest; silver money to attract income; water to attract rain at the right time.

It is also traditional for the women to decorate the floors with brightly coloured patterns, called *rangoli* patterns, made from natural products and dyes such as rice-flour and water, dry powders, spices and chalks. The patterns are free and swirly and are based on flower and leaf shapes.

Diwali: Festival of Lights. Children light candles beside framed picture of a goddess.

Some traders regard Diwali as the start of a new financial year; they settle all their bills, close their account books and start new ones. As a sign of good will, they also pay courtesy calls on business associates. It is also a time to visit members of the family. Those who have had a good year thank Lakshmi for her blessing and those who have not pray that she will bring them greater success in the year to come.

In common with the celebration of many festivals in all religions, cards and presents are exchanged at Diwali time. The most common greeting inside a Diwali card is *Subh Diwali*, which means Happy Diwali, and the words 'best wishes for the year to come' may be added in either language. The cards may bear pictures of Lakshmi or of *diwa* lamps. Gifts are also given to tradesmen; children receive gifts of sweets. Indeed shops display pyramids of brightly coloured sweets, some of which are wrapped in edible silver paper. The more expensive sweets are made of boiled milk and sugar, flavoured with nuts, fruit, raisins and rosewater, the cheaper ones of spun sugar and roasted corn.

Diwa lamps such as the above are used to decorate a house.

In India, as part of the celebration, there are the *melas* (fairs) to go to which include rides and hot, spicy or sweet, sticky snacks. There are also entertainers, perhaps snake charmers, camel and elephant rides and many side-shows. Traders sell animals and farm produce, books, bangles, toys and clothes. If possible, everyone has new clothes for

Diwali. There may be firework displays, which particularly recall the victory in battle of Rama over Ravana. In Britain such *melas* have to be adapted to the climate and availability of premises and entertainers. In areas where there are many Hindus, there may be a Hindu centre at which festivities can take place. An evening's entertainment with food, sweets, music and worship is usually arranged to mark the festival. The centrepiece for such an event might well be an enactment of the Rama and Sita story or at least readings from the *Ramayana.* A Hindu lady might interpret the story in dance to the accompaniment of a sitar or small harmonium.

Thematic approaches to Diwali

If there are Hindu children in your class and/or you have introduced Hinduism to the class before, you may wish to treat the topic in isolation, looking at Diwali as a major festival in the Hindu calendar and drawing out the main concepts. In a predominantly Christian class Diwali might be studied as part of a theme, particularly one which links with Christianity. Three possible thematic approaches are suggested below.

Light (Level One)

To start in the experience of the child, the theme of light could be used and its importance emphasised, before moving on to show the significance of light in the festival.

The emphasis on light could develop into a study of Diwali alongside other festivals where light features predominantly, such as Christmas or Chanukah. Light in such contexts is often symbolic of good and of God: 'I am the light of the world', Jesus is reported as saying; 'Whoever follows me will have the light of life and will never walk in darkness' (John 8:12). Referring to Jesus John 1:4, 5 reads: 'The Word was the source of life, and this life brought light to mankind. The light shines in the darkness, and the darkness has never put it out' (*Good News Bible).* Jesus is seen by Christians as showing the way to live, as being a force for good in an evil world.

At Chanukah the Jews recall a time when they recaptured their Temple from King Antiochus and relit the Temple oil lamps to symbolise the presence of God. There was only enough oil to last one night but, by a miracle, the oil lasted for eight days and nights. The festival of Chanukah lasts for eight days and the Jews light the candles on their menorah at home to remind them that the light of the spirit burns even against the odds.

Our day-to-day use and need of light provides another direction in which to explore the topic. Examples such as how we need light to see, how plants need it for growth etc. abound. You might wish to move on to consider what it would be like without light and do a study of blindness. The work of the Royal National Institute for the Blind and local projects for the blind could form a part of such a project.

Lynne Scholefield, *Chanukah* (Living Festivals Series; RMEP, 1983)
Nigel Hunter, *Helen Keller* (Great Lives Series; Wayland, 1985)
RNIB North Region, Hartley Hill, North Street, Leeds 2. Tel. Leeds 456443

A New Start (Level Two)

At Diwali homes are cleaned, accounts paid and new clothes bought. Effectively a new year is started spiritually and financially. This aspect of the festival can be extended to include creative work about new things – presents, clothes, shoes etc. and how we celebrate the new year in Great Britain, particularly Scotland, and how it is celebrated by the Chinese and the Jews (Rosh Hashanah). The theme could be extended to a study of new life in the spring and from there to Easter and the meaning of Christ's resurrection for Christians.

Living Festivals Series (RMEP):
    Chinese New Year by Anne Bancroft (1984)
    Easter by Norma Fairbairn and Jack Priestley (1982)

A link with Rosh Hashanah

Although the Jewish new year festival takes place in autumn when plants are dying, it is nevertheless all about life. This is because the Jews believe that God is a God of life and that spring will come again. Unlike the riotous British celebrations of the new year in January, the Jewish celebration of the new year in the seventh month of the Jewish Calendar (Tishri) is quiet and contemplative. It is time for looking back as well as forward.

According to Jewish legend, Rosh Hashanah is also the anniversary of the creation of Adam and the birthday of Abraham, Isaac and Jacob. The mood is serious and solemn, and Jews will look at themselves and assess their life and shortcomings – a kind of spiritual stock-taking and an opportunity for renewal.

Rosh Hashanah is a holiday and a time of rest. There is a feast at which bread is dipped in honey and eaten, as people exchange the greeting: 'May it be a sweet and good year'. The *shofar* (ram's horn) is blown at the morning service to call the Jews to attention. The Talmud (a collection of commentaries relating to the Mishnah, which is a selection of oral teaching based on the Torah and passed down by Jewish elders) says that when the shofar is blown at Rosh Hashanah, God gets up from his throne of justice and sits on his throne of mercy because he knows that his people want another chance and he wants to give it to them. After ten days comes Yom Kippur (the Day of Atonement) when adult Jews fast and pray, often kneeling or prostrating themselves, which is unusual because Jews normally stand to pray. On this day of solemn rejoicing, when God's forgiveness permits a new start, the synagogue has white drapes and the rabbi wears white instead of black.

The triumph of good over evil (Level Two)

This theme is central to the understanding of Diwali, as the Rama and Sita story demonstrates. On Diwali the Hindus settle not only accounts but also personal differences. Once Diwali has been looked at thoroughly, the theme of good triumphing over evil can be looked at in children's literature (some examples given below). In discussion children will doubtless have anecdotes about television programmes that demonstrate the concept. There is plenty of scope for imaginative and creative work. Older children can write and act out stories where the 'goodies' beat the 'baddies', particularly where it shows that taking a stance for good has resulted in triumph.

L. Frank Baum, *The Wizard of Oz* (Puffin, 1985)
Christianna Brand, *Nurse Matilda* (Knight Books, 1964)
S. Hoff, *Stanley* (World's Work, 1978)
Ted Hughes, *The Iron Man* (Faber, 1968)
C. S. Lewis, *The Lion, the Witch and the Wardrobe* (Collins, 1974)
Ursula Moray-Williams, *Jessie the Burglar's Cat* (Puffin, 1983)

Ursula Moray-Williams, *The Adventures of the Little Wooden Horse* (Puffin, 1959)

K. M. Peyton, *Froggett's Revenge* (OUP, 1985)

A Link with Easter

To forge a link with Christianity and indeed move on to a festival which is usually dealt with in the school calendar, this concept of the triumph of good over evil can be picked up in a study of Easter. Jesus's conquering of death is a story, whether or not you take it literally, of good triumphing over evil, life over death. The same theme appears in the Jewish festival of Purim and the Hindu festival of Holi (see Chapters 5 and 6). For accounts of the events leading up to and including the death and resurrection of Jesus, read Mark 14, 15 and 16 and related passages in the other gospels.

Creating a Diwali classroom

It is worth giving some thought to reorganising the classroom for the duration of this topic. Indian music playing quietly in the background and joss sticks burning can help to create an Indian atmosphere, though it may be preferable to restrict this to the more practical and less formal activities. To give focus to the work and to allow for an added experiential dimension, two areas of the room could be reconstructed: one as a family shrine and the other as an Indian grocer's shop. A shrine can be made by draping a table or shelf with a brightly coloured piece of cloth or sari and standing on it photos or statues of any of the Hindu gods. Fresh flowers, if possible, and tinsel add to the effect. As the topic evolves, garlands, diwa lamps and the puja tray can be added. The shrine is a simple way of bringing a visual element into the classroom and showing an important feature of the Hindu home. The shop corner can be constructed on a table using a till, cardboard or plastic money and empty tins and packets. Then products can be priced in rupees or sterling (as appropriate to the simulated coins provided) and trading can take place whenever it is convenient in the school day. Another reason for the shop corner is that since there are Indian grocers' shops in Great Britain, the shop may provide a link to children's experience; it also leads nicely into the custom of settling accounts (see p. 78).

Another possibility is to drape a sari around a tailor's dummy or a cardboard model of an Indian woman which you might be able to obtain from a travel agent (see p. 48).

Suggested activities

A study of Diwali can fall into two neat parts — what is being celebrated and how it is celebrated. It may be necessary to make a short general study of Hinduism by way of introduction if this is the first time the children have come across this religion. If this is the case, take some of the material and tasks suggested in Chapters 2 and 3 on family life and worship. Other than that and the setting up of the classroom, it is probably best to start with the story of Rama and Sita.

What is being celebrated

This story is the kind that children will love, full of drama and tension. It could be told in its entirety or in daily instalments. Depending upon their age and ability, pupils can write the story from memory, use worksheets, or write captions to drawn illustrations of each episode. Some might like to depict the story in cartoon form. A class frieze showing one scene or a series of events can be made with or without written accompaniment.

This is an example of a poem inspired by the story of Rama and Sita.

> *Ravana*
> Evil-eyed wicked man
> with lots of heads and plenty of arms
> Causing trouble wherever he goes
> Has no friends but plenty of foes.
> Caroline Copeland, aged eight.

How it is celebrated

There are so many aspects to celebrating Diwali that it is worth either mentioning only a few or summarising them on a pictorial worksheet. You could also point out the similarities between these ways of celebrating and the ways in which Christians celebrate Christmas, e.g.

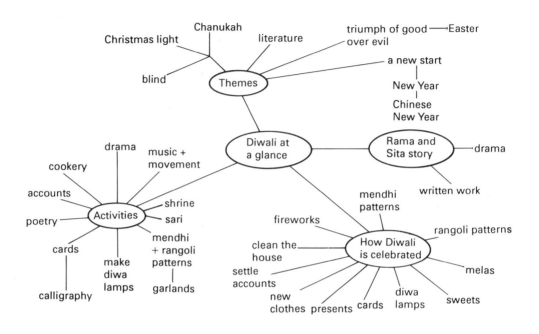

with parties, cards, presents and lights. Certain activities will follow
from this and could run concurrently with the work on the story.

Diwali floor patterns.

Diwa lamps

These can be made with clay if facilities allow, otherwise plasticine. Just
mould into shape (see p. 68) and float a cottonwool wick in oil or use a
small night light. If made of clay, the lamps can be decorated with
flowing patterns typical of Indian art.

Rangoli patterns

In India rangoli patterns are often drawn outside in the ground or on the
mud floor of the living room. The patterns are made from coloured
chalks, rice flour and spices and inspired by the shapes of leaves and
flowers.

Using a piece of paper or card, glue and items such as lentils,
turmeric, white flour and chalk, pupils can create impressive patterns.

First, make a design in light pencil. Then spread glue over the lines
that are to be coloured first. Carefully sprinkle one of the powders over

74

this and blow or tip the card to get rid of the excess. Repeat this process for each colour or texture used, then fill in some of the spaces with coloured chalk. The chalk can either be ground up and sprinkled onto glue or used for drawing in the normal way.

The same sort of effects can be made with powder paints and large patterns done in this way look impressive on the classroom walls.

Typical rangoli patterns.

Mendhi patterns

At festival times, Indian women often paint one another's hands (see picture). Pupils can have fun doing this, perhaps in the sacred colours of red and orange.

Typical mendhi patterns.

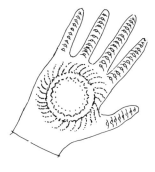 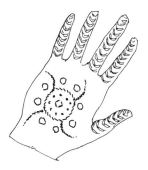 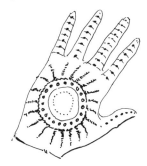

Garlands

Garlands are made for decoration and to wear at celebrations. They can be made from tissue paper in the traditional, festive colours of red and orange. Extension work could involve using these colours for a colour table or as a colour theme for display or for fabric printing.

75

Diwali cards

The greeting inside Diwali cards is usually *Subh Diwali*, meaning Happy Diwali and implying wishes for the year ahead. Such cards may be illustrated with a diwa lamp or one of the gods, particularly Lakshmi, and flowers.

Calligraphy

A Hindu prayer, with particular relevance to Diwali, such as the one below, could be written out as a handwriting exercise and perhaps decorated in the style of rangoli patterns. This could be used as the front of a Diwali card.

> Lead us from evil to good,
> From unreality to reality,
> From death to immortality,
> From darkness to light.

Food

Eating is a distinctive part of any festival – and eating sweets is particularly characteristic of Diwali. A straightforward and popular activity is to make sweets to eat in class or at a Diwali party or to take home. If they are taken home, it is a nice idea to place them in a small box lined with coloured tissue paper or a paper serviette, perhaps sticking with the red and orange colour theme. They can look very attractive.

Indian sweets
225 g desiccated coconut
100 g icing sugar
200 g condensed milk (small can)
food colouring

METHOD
Mix all ingredients together, roll into balls, coat with icing sugar and leave to set.

If practical, you might also like to make a hot savoury dish in the classroom using a Calor Gas stove. The following vegetarian recipe comes from *Madhur Jaffrey's Indian Cookery* (BBC Publications, 1982):

Phool gobi aur aloo ki bhaji (Cauliflower with potatoes)
½ lb (225g) potatoes
1 medium sized cauliflower
5 tablespoons vegetable oil
1 teaspoon whole cumin
1 teaspoon ground cumin
½ teaspoon ground coriander
¼ teaspoon ground turmeric
¼ teaspoon cayenne pepper
½–1 fresh, hot green chilli, very finely chopped (optional)
½ teaspoon ground roasted cumin seeds (dry roast them in a
    frying pan)
1 teaspoon salt
freshly ground black pepper

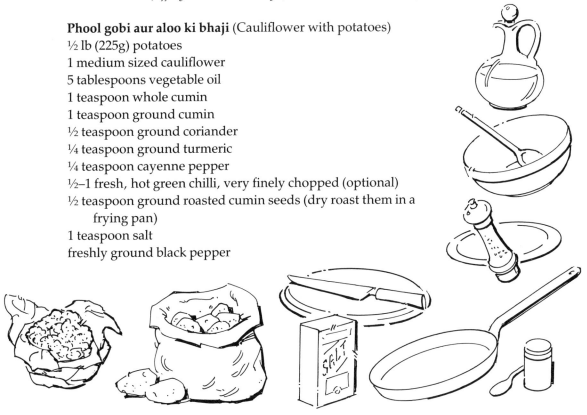

METHOD
Boil potatoes in jackets and allow to cool completely. (Potatoes that have been cooked the day before and refrigerated work well here.) Peel and dice them. Break cauliflower into florets and soak in water for 30 mins. Drain. Heat oil in large frying pan over medium flame. When hot, add whole cumin seeds. After 3–4 seconds, add cauliflower and cook for 2 mins, allowing it to brown in parts. Cover, turn the heat low and simmer for 4–6 mins until cauliflower is almost cooked but has some crispness left. Add diced potatoes, ground cumin, coriander, turmeric, cayenne, green chilli, ground roasted cumin, salt and some black pepper. Stir gently to mix. Continue to cook uncovered on low heat for another 3 mins or until potatoes are heated through. Stir gently.

Shrine and puja tray

A puja tray (silver with matching containers, sometimes available on loan from R.E. resource centres) can be laid at the shrine. It is possible to improvise by using a few small dishes. Put the traditional symbolic objects into the dishes (see p. 67).

Shop and accounts

To demonstrate the settling of accounts at Diwali time, the children can complete accounts sheets in a 'maths' session, setting out headings as follows:

NAME OF GOODS	WHAT I PAID FOR THEM £	WHAT I SOLD THEM FOR £

Music, movement and dance

If Hindu music can be obtained, various activities can be developed. Children can talk about the feelings aroused by the music, the rhythms and sounds they hear and the types of instruments used. Ideally, you may be able to borrow a sitar or harmonium to show in the classroom; otherwise show a poster or photograph.

The goddess
Sarasvati, playing
an Indian musical
instrument, the
veena.

Pupils can express their feelings about the music in movement,
perhaps dancing the Rama and Sita story. Music can also be used as
background for a narration or mime of the story.

If you decide to act out the Rama and Sita story, it can be done
effectively in episodes, using different groups of children for each, or it
can be staged as a continous drama using selected characters and a
'chorus' of monkeys. The full cast list includes: King Dasharatha,
Queens Kaushalya, Sumitra and Kaikeyi, Agni, Rama, Lakshmana,
Sita, Bharata, demon-deer, Hanuman and the monkeys, squirrel and
Ravana (who could be played by 10 children).

Each child can make a mask to depict the part he is playing. These might be elaborate papier-mâché affairs or a simple piece of card secured around the head with an elastic band.

Presentation or party

The topic could culminate in a presentation to the rest of the school and/ or parents or be celebrated in a class Diwali party, at which you could have:

- Displays of work
- Music and dance
- Indian food, sweets and biscuits
- Garlands as decorations
- Joss sticks for atmosphere
- A presentation of the Ramayana

BIBLIOGRPAHY

Howard Marsh, *Divali* (Living Festivals Series: Arnold Wheaton/RMEP, 1982)

Olivia Bennett, *Festival! Diwali* (Commonwealth Institute/Macmillan Education, 1987). With accompanying worksheets by Rosalind Kerven.

Joanna Troughton, *The Story of Rama and Sita* (Blackie)

Eric J. Sharpe, *Thinking about Hinduism* new ed. (Lutterworth, 1988)

K. M. Sen, *Hinduism* (Pelican, 1961)

Swami Yogeshananda, *The Way of the Hindu* (Hulton Educational, 1973)

USEFUL ADDRESSES

Commission for Racial Equality, Elliot House, 10/12 Allington Street, London SW1E 5EH (Tel: (071) 828 7022)

Minority Group Support Service, Southfields, South Street, Coventry CV1 5EJ (Tel: 0203 26888)

Resource centres

Sacred Trinity Centre, Chapel Street, Salford

The Hindu Centre, Edge Lane, Liverpool

The Hindu Centre, 39 Grafton Terrace, London NW5

Institute of Indian Culture, 44 Castletown Road, London W14 9HE

Articles of faith (Religious artefacts and resources for education)

Mrs C. M. Winstanley, Sacred Trinity Centre, Chapel Street, Salford.

The BBC children's programme 'Watch', aimed at 4- to 7-year-olds, regularly depicts religious festivals from many cultures and Diwali is one such. It is worth recording these as they are repeated and those concerning festivals are usually screened at the time the festival is celebrated. The BBC provides information packs for parents and teachers.

5 PURIM

Although a minor festival, Purim, which takes place in March, is possibly the most joyful one in Judaism. It is also the oddest. The story, which is found in the Old Testament Book of Esther, doesn't even mention God, yet it is a time for praising God for his goodness. The usual restrained behaviour in the synagogue is replaced by a near-rowdiness and the usual abstemious attitude toward alcohol gives way to revelling! Purim is a normal workday, yet it is also a festival. People celebrate in their homes as well as in the synagogue, as is usually the case with Jewish festivals. Many schools devote a whole day to celebrating Purim.

The Book of Esther tells of how Esther courageously acted to avert a scheme to slaughter all the Jews in Persia. Haman is the instigator of this scheme, and at the time of Purim the Jews remember all the 'Hamans' of the world – those who have tried to wipe out the Jews at some point in their history, the most recent and horrific of these being Hitler. But despite Hitler, despite Haman and many other persecutors, Judaism has survived. There is a strong sense of nationalism in the festival of Purim and, many argue, little of theological significance. Indeed, the historicity of the account is open to question. Yet even if the characters and events are fictitious, the meaning for the Jews is very real for there have been many attempts throughout history to destroy them. But Judaism continues to flourish, for which Jews thank God, especially at Purim.

The festival's name comes from the Persian word *pur,* meaning lots. This is because the evil Haman cast lots to determine the day that the Jews would die. The date was set for the 14th of Adar, which falls in March one month before Passover (Pesach). The story of Esther, full of drama and mystery, is as follows:

Esther

The king of Persia, Ahasuerus, had a beautiful wife named Vashti. Once, when the king was holding a banquet for his officials, he commanded that Vashti come to them as he was anxious to show her off to his guests. Vashti angered the king by refusing to come. His advisors told him that she must be punished because if she was allowed to disobey her husband then other wives in the land would do the same! They suggested that he get rid of her and choose another wife. The king accepted the advice and sent out officials to find as many beautiful young girls as possible and bring them back to the palace. The girls were looked after by a eunuch called Hegai who supervised the beauty treatments that were given to them in preparation for their being presented to the king. Hegai took a liking to Esther and looked after her especially well. Eventually she was the one that Ahasuerus chose to be his Queen.

Esther was Jewish, the cousin of a man called Mordecai, who had adopted her and brought her up after she was orphaned. Mordecai was appointed to an administrative position at the royal palace. He heard of a plot to kill the king, and warned the Queen, who in turn warned her husband. The plot was averted and a record of the incident written in the official records of the Persian Empire.

Then a man called Haman became the prime minister. Conceited and overbearing, he insisted that everyone bow down to him. As a Jew Mordecai would only bow down to God and not to men and refused to honour Haman in this way. Haman, furious, decided to kill all Jews in revenge and cast lots with his associates to determine on which day to carry out the massacre. The lot fell on the 13th day of the 12th month, Adar, which is March in our calendar.

Haman reported to the King that there were people in the land who did not obey his laws and who observed strange customs. He advised him to issue a decree throughout the empire to put these people, the Jews, to death, guaranteeing that their demise would bring 340,000 kilos of silver into the royal treasury. The king agreed and with his ring put the royal stamp of approval on the proclamation which ordered the slaughter.

When Mordecai heard of the proclamation he went into mourning in sackcloth and ashes. Esther, hearing from one of her servants that Mordecai was greatly distressed, sent to him to find out the cause. Mordecai sent her a copy of the proclamation and asked her to plead with the king to save the Jews. Esther replied that she could not just go to the king whenever she pleased or she might incur the death penalty; she had to wait until she was sent for, and the king had not sent for her for a month. Mordecai replied that if she did not go to the king, she would die anyway and that it was for just such a time as this that she had been made queen.

Esther, who wanted to help her people, was convinced. She asked Mordecai to gather some Jews together to fast and pray for her for three days and nights; she and her servant girl would be doing the same. Then she would seek an audience with the king, although it meant risking her life. After three days and nights of fasting and praying, Esther got ready in her most beautiful clothes and went to the inner court of the palace before the throning room. The king saw her and pointed his golden sceptre at her – a sign that she could enter his presence. He was so delighted by Esther that he told her she could make a request for anything, even for half his kingdom. Esther did not reply at once, instead she invited her husband and Haman to a banquet which she had prepared. During the banquet, Haman repeated the king's offer but Esther replied mysteriously that she would give him her answer the following night at another banquet she was preparing for her husband and Haman.

On his way home that night, Haman was in a good mood, but was irritated to see Mordecai outside the palace, who, as usual, did not bow to him. He went home and boasted to his wife and friends about his many sons and the high office that he held and the fact that he was due to dine again the following night with the king and queen. But he also grumbled that all this gave him no pleasure while Mordecai was around. So his wife and friends suggested that he should immediately have some gallows built and hang Mordecai. He could then go to the banquet happy. Haman welcomed this idea and had the gallows built.

That same night the king, unable to sleep, decided to read through the official records of the empire. He read about the plot to kill him which had been averted by Mordecai and realised that nothing had been done to honour his benefactor. He sent for Haman and told him that he wished to honour a man: how should he go about it? Haman, thinking that the man the king wished to honour was himself, suggested that he put royal robes on the man, mount him on a royal horse, and have him led by a nobleman throughout the city so that everyone could see him. The king ordered Haman to carry out the idea on Mordecai the Jew.

So to his great shame, Haman had to lead Mordecai through the city proclaiming to the people, 'See how the King rewards a man he wishes to honour'. When he went home, his family and friends added to his mortification by telling him that he was losing his power to Mordecai.

That night when Haman dined with the king and queen, Esther made her request. She asked that she and her people might live. She added, 'My people and I have been sold for slaughter. If it were nothing more serious than being sold into slavery, I would have kept quiet and not bothered you about it; but we are about to be destroyed – exterminated!' (Esther 7:4) (*Good News Bible*). Then the King asked, 'Who dares to do such a thing? Where is this man?' and Esther told him that it was Haman, who was seated with them. The king left the room in great distress and when he returned found Haman at Esther's feet begging for mercy. But he misread the scene and thought that Haman was trying to rape his wife. A couple of the king's assistants apprehended Haman and told the king, 'Haman even went so far as to build a gallows at his house so that he could hang Mordecai, who saved your majesty's life. It is twenty-two metres tall!' 'Hang Haman on it!' commanded the king.

Esther, who was given all of Haman's property, begged the

king to stop the slaughter of the Jews which was to take place on the 13th of Adar. The king said that what he had decreed could not be revoked as he had set his seal on it, but he gave Esther and Mordecai the authority and his royal seal to write their own instructions to all the provinces. So letters went out instructing that the Jews defend themselves from the attack in whatever way they saw fit. Thus when the day came, the Jews fought bloody battles and won through. Haman's ten sons were all slaughtered and on the 14th and 15th of Adar the fighting stopped and the Jews celebrated. Mordecai, who was now a powerful man in the royal court, instructed the people of the Persian empire to celebrate every year on the 14th and 15th of Adar. This tradition continues today for Jews throughout the world.

How the Jews celebrate Purim

Purim is celebrated in a synagogue service during which the scroll of the book of Esther, the *Megillah*, is read out. Every time the name Haman occurs, the children try to drown it by stamping, shaking rattles, banging tin lids and shouting 'May his name be blotted out'. This is not a vengeful attack on Haman, but a dismissal of him as a person worth nothing. After the service, there may be a fancy dress party at which gifts are exchanged. The disguises may be biblical, but not necessarily. Jewish schools spend much of the day in celebration, with fancy dress, talent contests and games. The fancy dress tradition is about 400 years old and may have been taken from the Christian custom of masquerading during the week before Lent, which comes around the same time.

At home there may be a special meal with the three-cornered cakes called *hamantaschen* — meaning Haman's ears. There are often collections for charities, and personal gifts are given to individuals in need and their families. Over a hundred years ago the Jews of New York began the Purim Association, which held a Purim ball every year to raise money for various charities. It is now the New York Federation of Philanthropies, one of the largest charities in the world.

Purim
celebrations.

Thematic approaches to Purim

As the main theme is praising God for the deliverance of the Jews from
an evil plot, a study of Purim would follow on nicely from a study of
Diwali, or Holi, picking up on the theme of good triumphing over evil.

As well as being full of fun and joy, Purim is a festival which
adequately demonstrates the strong sense of nationalism within
Judaism. Since it has no obvious links with anything in Christianity, it
would best be studied once the children have been introduced to
Judaism and are aware already of some of their customs and beliefs (see
Chapters 2 and 3).

For further information on Purim, read the book of Esther in the
Bible. Also useful is *When a Jew Celebrates* by Harry Gersh (Behrman
House, 1971). Jewish books and artefacts are available from Jewish
Education Bureau, 8 Westcombe Avenue, Leeds. Send SAE for
catalogue and price list.

Suggested tasks

1. *Recording the story*

There are many ways of recording the story of Esther: the method chosen will depend upon the age and abilities of the children concerned. For young children, pictorial worksheets with a space for the child's written commentary or short sentence may be best. Older and more able children may be able to record the story in their own words, particularly if the story is told in episodes so that there is less to remember at each stage. Some children might like to record the story in cartoon form or as a class collage.

2. *Calligraphy*

This English translation of a children's Hebrew song could be copied in best or decorated handwriting and perhaps displayed.

> Purim am I, Purim am I,
> All goodness and good cheer,
> But only once a year do I
> Come visiting you here.
> Hurray Purim, Hurray Purim,
> Drums beat and cymbals chime,
> Oh what a shame the feast can't last
> For one or two months' time!

Or this short prayer:

> *We thank God for saving Esther and Mordecai and all the Jewish people from the evil Haman who wanted to destroy us all.*

3. *Cookery*

Hamantaschen ('Haman's ears') can be made by using risen yeast dough or biscuit dough. For making in school, a packet mix will do.

INGREDIENTS FOR FILLING
2 cups of poppyseeds (variations are nuts and/or raisins)
1 cup of water or milk
½ cup honey
¼ cup sugar
large pinch of salt
2 eggs

METHOD

To make the filling, mix all the ingredients except the eggs in a saucepan and cook over moderate heat until thick. Allow to cool and add thoroughly beaten eggs. If too thin, cook gently for 1–2 mins. Add the variations, if required.

Roll the dough into circles 4 in. diameter and ¼–½ in. thick. Place a ball of filling in each one, moisten the edges and bring three 'sides' together to form a triangle. Pinch the seams together to seal. Brush the tops with diluted egg yolks or milk. Bake for 30–40 mins at 350°F (177°C, gas Mark 4) till lightly browned.

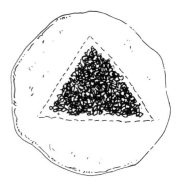

4. *Masks and puppets*

The story of Esther can be acted by the children or done as a puppet play. The main characters – Esther, Ahasuerus, Haman, Mordecai, and perhaps Vashti – need to be made and a puppet theatre constructed.

A simple way of making puppets is to use a paper plate, a cardboard tube (from kitchen roll for example) and bits of material, buttons and wool. Fix the tube across one edge of the plate with staples, then drape it with fabric for clothes. The fabric can be secured with staples, rubber bands and glue. Use buttons or bottle tops for the eyes, fabric for the other facial features and wool for the hair.

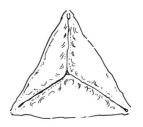

Hamantaschen.

Of course, puppets can be made in all sorts of more elaborate ways, and the story of Purim could be fitted into a craft topic on puppetry rather than the other way around.

Another method of dramatising the story is by using masks. These can be made from papier-mâché or clay, attached to sticks and held by the children in front of their own faces in the manner of the ancient Greeks. Older children can write their own scripts, while younger ones might mime to a narration.

5. *Presentation*

The topic could be presented in some way to the rest of the school, and indeed the parents, or celebrated within the classroom. For instance, a play could be performed and the children (and guests) could eat the *Hamantaschen*. To simulate the Jewish way of celebrating, children could be allowed to wear fancy dress. This might be restricted to dress relating to the story, if preferred.

The class might also like to organise a fund-raising event for a favourite charity, just as the Jews do at this time.

6. *Follow-up work*

If there are any Jewish schools nearby, you might find that they welcome visitors and you could take your Purim celebrations there. This might also be a good time to visit a synagogue and move on to a study of religious buildings or worship.

With older juniors a study of the oppression of the Jews might be worthwhile, particularly in relation to Hitler's regime. *The Diary of Anne Frank* would be a useful resource book in this case. This project could be extended to look at other forms of oppression – of blacks in South Africa, for example.

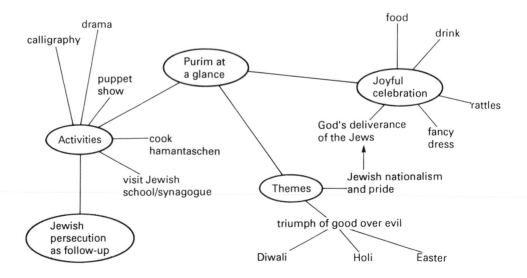

BIBLIOGRAPHY

Vanora Leigh, *Anne Frank* (Great Lives Series; Wayland, 1985)

A. Bull, *Anne Frank* (Hamish Hamilton, 1984)

I. H. Birnie, *Trevor Huddleston* (SCM Press, 1984)

Faith in Action Series (RMEP):

    R. J. Owen, *I Wish He Were Black* (Trevor Huddleston) (1978)

    R. J. Owen, *Free at Last* (Martin Luther King) (1980)

6 HOLI

Halfway through the last month of the Hindu calendar, Phalgun, around March or April, is the festival of Holi. As it is the end of one growing season and the start of another, people feel that they have something to look forward to: bonfires are lit and there is much boisterous merry-making. It marks a new start for farmers, just as Diwali marks a new financial year for traders and professional people.

There are several stories associated with Holi, the most common one concerning a man called Prahlad.

The Story of Prahlad

PRAHLAD WAS a prince in north-east India, well known for being devout in his worship of Vishnu. Prahlad's father, King Hiranya-Kasipu, was as evil as his son was holy; he issued a decree that everyone should worship the king rather than any god. Prahlad refused to obey this command, at which his father angrily vowed to do anything he could to force his son to abandon his religion and worship him. He ordered that his son be tied to a pillar and beaten, but this did not make Prahlad change his mind. So he put the prince with a mad elephant in a walled yard. Rather than trample him to death, the elephant became calm and peaceful in Prahlad's presence as Prahlad whispered the names of the gods. The king next ordered that his son be thrown from a high cliff into the deep pool just below the palace. But Prahlad survived this ordeal too. Legend has it that the mark on the rocks above a pool in the Janxi district of India is Prahlad's footprint. To this day pilgrims visit the site.

The King was determined to get the better of his son and turned for help to his daughter Holika, a sorceress. One of Holika's magical powers was an ability to walk unharmed through flames, so she gave instructions for a huge fire to be made, and when it was burning fiercely, she grabbed hold of

Prahlad and leapt into the fire with him. There were dreadful screams, which shocked the onlookers, but they came from Holika, who had not known that her magic only worked when she entered fire alone. Prahlad was unharmed, saved by his trust in God. At this, King Hiranya-Kasipu finally gave up, repented of his sins and never again tried to persuade his son to abandon his faith.

In the areas where the story is remembered, the bonfires are a reminder of the death of the wicked Holika. The tradition of making a lot of noise at Holi is said to recall another story about the sorceress. She frightened people so much that they gave in to her demands to have a child to eat every day. One day, at the suggestion of a wise man, all the mothers gathered at a certain spot and stood against Holika when she came along. They hurled insults and screamed at her so much that she ran away and never bothered them again.

The significance of Holi

Like the story of Rama and Sita celebrated at Diwali, the story of Prahlad celebrates the triumph of good over evil. Linked to this is the celebration of loyalty to one's beliefs even when it involves great stress and danger. On a simpler level, Holi can be regarded as a festival linked with harvest and spring.

How Hindus celebrate Holi

In rural India, where mass media entertainment is rare, a festival is a good excuse for having fun. Some areas may organise processions and talent contests. They may put on a play of their own or hire professional entertainers.

Holi is particularly popular among young men and boys, who begin collecting for the bonfires at the beginning of Phalgun. In some parts of India, they raise funds to pay for the festivities by performing traditional dances in the streets.

The day before the night of the full moon, Hindus fast in preparation for the festival. At dusk, the priest lights the bonfire, says special prayers and the celebrations begin. The men and boys dance around the fires and some jump over and through them. There is a lot of noise with horns blowing, drums beating and much singing and shouting.

In rural areas of India, the harvested crops are offered to God by placing a portion in the fire: barley is roasted in the ashes to be eaten later; coconuts (symbols of fertility) are also roasted. Sugar canes with ears of corn and chick peas tied to them are dipped into the flames. At the end of the evening, some people take home a pot of the glowing embers with which to start their own Holi fires when they get home.

Throughout most of India the bonfire marks the start of boisterous activity and the spraying of coloured water. Not so in Nepal: there it signals the end. The week before the full moon, a pole called a Chir, decorated with strips of cloth, is erected. This is the sign for the fun associated with Holi to begin. On the day of the full moon, the pole is lowered and carried away to the bonfire. People grab at the pieces of cloth to keep as good luck charms.

Elsewhere, the fights with water and powder begin on the morning after the fire. These are quite unruly and many women will not venture out at this time for fear of being caught up in the riotous mobs. People exchange greetings with their friends and relatives, then return home at midday to eat a special meal.

In some areas there are processions of singers and dancers, pageants and dramatic presentations of the stories commemorated at Holi. In the evening, people don clean clothes and assemble in a park or other public place to eat and gossip. There is singing, perhaps a play and folk dances. Most of the dances tell religious stories, for example the *Ras Lila* dance, which is in honour of the early life of Krishna.

In general there are fairs and circuses, to which many non-Hindu Indians will also go: the madness and fun is irresistible. In this way Holi helps to break down barriers between people. Differences are forgotten, people patch up quarrels and pay or forgive debts. All classes, rich or poor, high or low, join in and people get a chance to tease those who are usually their superiors – all in good humour. Everyone wants to celebrate the joy and hope of the new season.

Thematic approaches to Holi

Holi as a new beginning (Level One)

Holi can be treated as a spring festival and/or a new year festival, particularly with infants. Any work on this can be put in the context of known celebrations for new year and observations of spring.

Let's take these ideas separately. First, in the context of spring, Holi could feature as a festival that occurs at this time. Hindus in Britain, though usually living in cities not in farming communities, celebrate

95

Holi, particularly in areas such as Coventry where there is a large Hindu population. However, the festivities concerning Holi will be more colourful in India than in the streets of England and there will be more significance attached to the agricultural side of things. It may, then, be necessary to put Holi into an Indian context. A study of spring involving plants, trees, buds, lambs, chickens and other forms of new life occurring at the end of winter will enhance to the children's experience and prepare them to understand the joy of the festival of Holi.

New year can be linked with Diwali and, as suggested in Chapter 4, also with the Jewish celebration of Rosh Hashanah and the Chinese new year.

Another suitable context for looking at Holi is harvest time and ideas for comparative study are given in Chapter 8, which particularly focuses on Christian harvest and the Jewish festival, Sukkot.

The triumph of good over evil (Level Two)

This recurrent theme can also be seen in the Jewish story of Purim, the Christian story of Easter and the Hindu festival of Diwali. As was suggested in the chapter on Diwali, it is a good idea to find examples of this concept in children's literature. Most children will be able to come up with examples of good overcoming bad in television programmes, e.g. Thundercats, Gobots, Spiderman, Superman and so on. Look out particularly for ideas showing victory of people who have held on to good principles. There is a list of suitable children's books on this theme on pp. 71–2.

Children can be encouraged, depending upon age and ability, to write their own stories illustrating the theme. Stories such as the one about Prahlad or Esther (Purim) or Rama and Sita (Diwali) or Jesus's death and resurrection can be introduced to show the religious element – that people act on their religious beliefs and that God looks after those who honour him.

Standing by one's beliefs (Level Two)

Drawing on the idea that Prahlad held fast to his love of Vishnu and did not give in despite the tortures he suffered, a study could be made of people of varying religions who have done the same, particularly in modern times. One such example is Dietrich Bonhoeffer, a Christian priest captured in the Second World War who, even in the face of torture, would not betray his friends or give up his Christian faith.

No Compromise (1983) by A. Constant in the RMEP Faith in Action Series tells the story of Dietrich Bonhoeffer.

Suggested tasks

1. *Setting the scene*
For a full project on Holi, to set the atmosphere, joss sticks and Indian music can be used and a part of the classroom set aside for Hindu artefacts or even a simulated family shrine. This area could be draped with a sari or brightly coloured fabric and posters of the god Vishnu and scenes depicting celebrations of Holi.

2. Act out the story of Prahlad in mime or dance. Some pupils could narrate it. Of course, there would be practical difficulties in acting out the part with real fire! If the medium of dance is used, some children can be flames and overcome Holika while lifting Prahlad aloft as the conqueror. The story could be recorded by the children in their own words with illustrations, or as a class wall frieze with appropriate captions.

3. Food is a popular aspect of any such topic work and the smells of the spices are evocative of the Hindu culture. For the recipe below you will need access to a kitchen or a Calor Gas stove. At least let the children smell some spices if they do not cook with them. Spices typically used in Indian food such as garam masala, turmeric, coriander, cumin, chilli, cayenne pepper, garlic can be obtained at most supermarkets. If not, the local delicatessen or health food shop will stock them.

RECIPE

Gajar, matar, aur aloo ki bhaji
(Carrots, peas and potatoes, flavoured with cumin)

6 oz (175 g) carrots
6 oz (175 g) potatoes, boiled, drained and cooled
6 oz (175 g) onions
1 spring onion

3 tablespoons mustard oil (or any vegetable oil)
1½ teaspoons whole cumin seeds
2 whole, dried red-hot chillies
6 oz (175 g) shelled peas
1 teaspoon salt
¼ teaspoon sugar

METHOD

Peel carrot and cut into ¼-inch dice. Do the same with potatoes. Coarsely chop onion. Cut spring onion into very thin slices. Heat oil in large frying pan over medium flame. When hot, put in cumin seeds and allow to sizzle for 3–4 seconds. Add chopped onion and stir and cook for 5 mins or until onion pieces turn translucent. Add carrots and peas and stir for about a minute. Cover, turn heat to low and cook for about 5 mins until vegetables are tender. Uncover and turn heat up slightly. Add chillies, potatoes, salt and sugar. Stir and cook for 2–3 mins. Add spring onion. Stir and cook for 30 seconds. Remove whole chillies before serving.

From *Madhur Jaffrey's Indian Cookery* (BBC Publications, 1982)

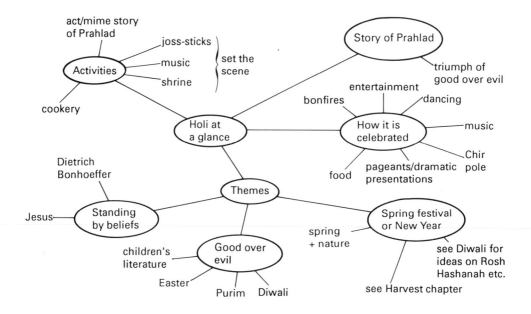

BIBLIOGRAPHY

Janis Hannaford, *Holi* (Living Festivals Series; RMEP, 1983)

V. P. (Hemant) Kanitkar, *Hindu Stories* (Religions of the World Series; Wayland, 1986)

The books on Hinduism recommended in the chapter on Diwali. There are also useful addresses given at the end of that chapter.

7 RAMADAN AND EID-UL-FITR

Ramadan is an important month in the Muslim calendar. It is not a festival but a fast, at the end of which is a festival called Eid-ul-fitr, a cheerful celebration. Ramadan highlights the Muslims' devotion to Allah and celebrates one of the five pillars of their faith: fasting. The giving of the Qur'an to Muhammad is also commemorated at this time. Because of the lunar calendar that Muslims adhere to, Ramadan can fall at any time of the year and will gradually work its way through the Western calendar.

During Ramadan, devout Muslims will abstain from food, drink and sex during the hours of daylight. Depending on the time of year that the fast falls, this could be for many hours. Young children do not have to fast totally, but will do without snacks and sweets. When they are older, they will miss a meal and then, from the age of twelve, will fast like the adults. Pregnant women, the very old, and the ill are also

A night meal during Ramadan.

exempted from fasting. Because they must remember the less fortunate at this time, some families invite less well off people to dine with them after sunset and banquets for lonely and/or poor people are held at some mosques.

During the period of the fast, Muslims focus their attention upon their religion. They give thanks for the Qur'an and try to read it all, one-thirtieth each day. It is in obedience to God's command in the Qur'an that Muslims fast. Fasting helps them to avoid excess and to remember God's goodness to them for which they must give him thanks. Finally, it helps the prosperous Muslim to identify with the poor and to remember to help them. If they do not share their belongings and kindness with those less fortunate their fast is not acceptable to God. Giving to the poor (*zakat*) is one of the five pillars of Islamic faith.

On one night during Ramadan Muslims especially remember the time that the Angel Gabriel gave the holy scriptures to Muhammad. That night is called 'Lailat-al-Qadr', the Night of Power.

Ramadan at the Southall Mosque in London.

In Muslim countries, school and work days can be adjusted so that people can get some sleep. If the nights are short, there may not be much time for sleep between the evening meal and the morning meal. In Britain there is no such allowance and people must carry on as normal, despite being hungry and tired. It is worth emphasising the commitment involved in rising 45 minutes before dawn to eat a meal – and even earlier for the women of the family who normally prepare the food.

Eid-ul-fitr

Eid-ul-fitr begins as soon as the Muslims see the new moon on the last evening of Ramadan and celebrations last for three days. Everyone has new clothes, if possible; there are parties, special food and children receive presents and money. Sweets and cakes are taken to friends and relatives, greetings cards are sent and money given to charities.

On the morning of the first day of Eid, Muslims attend the mosque. Sometimes the poor gather outside the mosques and beg for alms. Later on there are fairs and entertainments. Families also remember their dead relations and friends and visit their graves.

Planning suggestions

A project on Ramadan and its background is probably best carried out over a period of time – at least two weeks. Because the activities suggested below permeate the curriculum, it is easy to have a 'Ramadan fortnight' without disrupting the timetable balance. Alternatively, the project can be fitted into the topic work slot of the timetable.

The topic – Starting off

If this is the first time the subject of Islam has been touched upon, it is a good idea to show where in the world Muslims live. A world map on the wall focuses the children's attention and shows the extent of Islamic influence. The main areas of Islam are Pakistan, Turkey, Iran, Iraq, Saudi Arabia, Bangladesh, Syria, Egypt, Israel, Morocco, Libya, Tunisia and Algeria. England has a large Muslim community of around one million. The children will also need to see pictures of Muslims and mosques. Posters and slides are available from local teachers' centres and the Islamic Foundation (see p. 110). They will also need to become familiar with some new words: Islam, Muslim, Allah and Mosque. These can be reinforced in question and answer sessions, but also in games. The simplest involves making a few cardboard 'jigsaws' (see below) with statements such as: 'The people of Islam are called . . .', 'Muslims worship in a . . .', 'Muslims call God . . .', etc.

Worksheets to colour and complete also help to familiarise the children with new words and concepts. Very young children can make sentences using the 'Breakthrough to Literacy' scheme with the new vocabulary added.

Note: It is worth emphasizing the following points:

(1) The Muslims call God Allah, but this does not mean that they are worshipping a different God from Christians or Jews.

(2) The religion is called Islam and its adherents are called Muslims.

(3) No representations of God or Muhammad are permitted in Islamic art.

Thematic approach to Ramadan

At Lent many Christians give up certain foods, such as sweets, as a sacrifice to God. They renew their faith and pray to try to be better Christians. In this they follow the example of Jesus who fasted in the wilderness for 40 days and nights while praying that God would reveal his will to him. They also remember the need to give to the poor. The Jewish New Year festival, Rosh Hashanah, culminates in a day of fasting called Yom Kippur (notes on this can be seen in the Diwali chapter, p. 71).

With older children Ramadan could be treated as part of a theme on fasting and self-denial. With infants, it is worth making a link with Pancake Tuesday and Lent, if they have been dealt with during the school year, because this relates to their experience and shows a common theme in Christianity and Islam. Such young children will not really understand the concept of self-denial, but they can still look at how Muslims observe Ramadan and celebrate Eid-ul-fitr. The fact that they deny themselves food indicates how seriously the Muslims take their devotion to God.

A display of Eid cards.

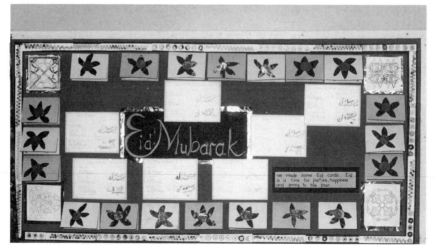

Activities

1. *Make an Eid card*
Choose an Islamic design or flower for the front, which can be drawn on or cut out and stuck on. Write *Eid Mubarak* inside, meaning Happy Eid. Older children might like to write out the prayer below:

> O, Allah, the Merciful and the Benevolent,
> Teach us the meaning of Eid
> And make us more like thee
> And give us understanding
> Enough to make us kind
> So we may judge all people
> With our heart and not our mind.

2. *Calligraphy*
Write *Eid Mubarak* in Urdu and Arabic. This can be done individually or as a large class display. Young children, who would have difficulty with writing this, could colour in the Urdu lettering and join the dots of the Arabic lettering on a worksheet. A possible activity for older children would be to copy out the Eid prayer and decorate it.

3. *Make food*
Make Turkish delight and Indian shortbread (recipes given on p. 107) and pack into small boxes covered in shiny gold and blue sweet papers.

4. *Hold an Eid party*
This is a good activity for the last day of the project. In keeping with the colour theme, blue and yellow balloons could be used to decorate the classroom and place mats made in these colours for the tables. An effective place mat can be made from two circles of paper, one blue and one of yellow. Fold the yellow piece into four and cut shapes from it. Stick it over the blue circle and you have a patterned place mat.

   Eat the food made in cookery classes and play some Islamic music for background atmosphere. The children could even dress in Islamic clothes.

5. *Give to the poor*
Hold a fund-raising event or take a collection for a local charity.

   Tasks from Chapters 2 and 3 on family life and worship could be used to augment this topic, especially if no previous work on Islam has been done. Colourful tasks that could be useful in this case include making a wall frieze of mosques against the sunset (see p. 56), making a class prayer mat (p. 59) and dressing up with saris (p. 48).

Discussion based on activities

LEVEL ONE

1. How might it feel to fast?

Young children can be prompted here by thinking first about missing crisps at break, then one meal and so on. A further prompt is to imagine a hot playtime and then not being able to have a glass of water. The children can enter into the spirit of Ramadan if their snacks – crisps, biscuits, milk, etc. – are delayed for ten minutes.

2. What would you have the most difficulty in giving up?

This question can help children to appreciate the seriousness with which the Muslims take their religion. Remember that even though children do not fast, they may be required to give up sweets and snacks.

LEVEL TWO

3. What might be the practical effects of fasting? How would it affect daily lives, their work, efficiency and family routines? (Note that some people fast occasionally for health reasons.)

4. How do you think fasting helps people to focus upon God and their religion?

Written work could be set as an extension of the discussion.

RECIPES

Turkish delight

1 lb/450 g granulated sugar
1 teaspoon lemon juice
1 oz/25 g powdered gelatine
4 drops vanilla essence
1 oz/25 g pistachio nuts, halved
1 tablespoon rosewater
3 drops food colouring
1 oz/25 g icing sugar
1 oz/25 g cornflour

METHOD

Grease a tin 6 in./15 cm square with butter. In a pan, dissolve sugar in ½ pint/250 ml water. Add lemon juice; bring to boil until mixture forms a hard ball when dropped in cold water or when 120°C/250°F is reached on a sugar thermometer. Remove from the heat, leave to stand for 10 mins. Dissolve gelatine in ¼ pint/125 ml hot water and stir into mixture with essence, nuts, rosewater and colouring. Pour into tin. Leave to set overnight. Cut into squares. Toss in icing sugar and cornflour.

Indian shortbread

¾ cup castor sugar
1 cup ghee (or soft margarine)
1 egg
2 teaspoons baking powder
pinch bicarbonate of soda
¼ teaspoon nutmeg
¼ teaspoon cinnamon
2½ cups flour
blanched almonds

METHOD

Put ghee in bowl. Add baking powder, sugar and spices. Stir briskly with spoon. Add egg. Stir till frothy. Add flour to make dough. Divide into balls, snooker-ball sized. Roll between palms and flatten with fingers until ½ inch thick. Place a blanched whole almond in the middle of each circle. Bake in medium oven to pale cream colour. Allow to cool before removing from baking tray.

107

A story to use with your class

Three Dates

AISHA, the Blessed Prophet's wife, was a very hospitable person. She loved to entertain guests and spend happy hours chatting to them. Once, a woman came to visit Aisha, bringing her two daughters with her. Aisha received her, smiling and welcoming, and very soon the two women were deep in conversation. However, Aisha was faced with a certain difficulty. She wanted to entertain her guest, but at that time things were very hard in Medina. Often the people went hungry, and in the Blessed Prophet's house no fire was made for days on end. It was difficult to come by the simplest food: even dates were in short supply.

Aisha decided that she must search the house thoroughly in the hope of finding something to offer her guest. The room in which she had welcomed her guest was so small that when Aisha stood up her head almost touched the ceiling. It did not take Aisha very long to search it, and she quickly realised that she did not have very much to offer her guest. Eventually, though, she managed to find three dates. Aisha gave them to her guest, who looked at her very gratefully.

The woman gave one date to each of her daughters, and the girls grabbed them eagerly. They were very hungry and had not had enough to eat for several days. Their mother kept one date for herself, but she did not eat it. Instead, she held it in her hand while she went on talking to Aisha.

Because they were hungry, the two little girls gobbled up their dates very quickly. When they had finished, they began to eye the last date, the one which their mother held in her hand. Their mother saw them out of the corner of her eye, and she smiled. She knew exactly what they wanted, and what she must do. So, she divided the last date into two pieces and gave half to each of the girls.

Aisha was very moved by the great love and self-sacrifice shown by this mother, and as soon as the Blessed Prophet came home, she told him what had happened.

'Indeed', the Blessed Prophet said. 'The woman has entered Paradise because of the love and kindness she showed to her little daughters. Allah will show her mercy because she showed mercy to them.'

From *Love at Home* by Khurram Murad (Islamic Foundation 1983).

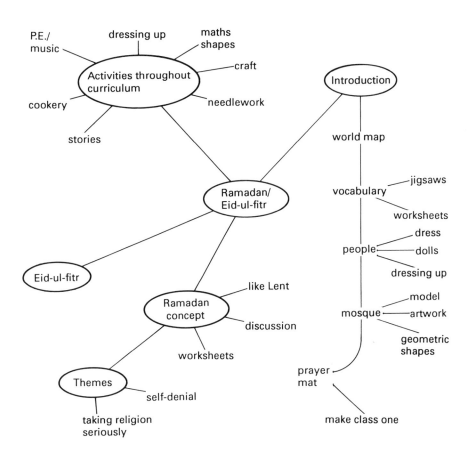

BIBLIOGRAPHY AND ADDRESSES

Janis Hannaford, *Ramadan and Eid-ul-fitr* (Living Festivals Series; RMEP, 1982)

Mardijah Aldrich Tarantino, *Marvellous Stories from the Life of Muhammad* (1986)

Ahmad Von Denffer, *Islam for Children* (1986)

The last two books are both published by the Islamic Foundation, 223 London Road, Leicester. The foundation also sells slides, books and posters. Send for a catalogue.

The Slide Centre, 143 Chatham Road, London SW11 6SR

The ATV series 'Believe It Or Not' has a programme introducing Islam. The series is repeated fairly often. The commentary is aimed at older children, but you could show it on video and stop now and again to explain and point things out.

Posters, clothes and other artefacts may be obtained from your local teachers' centre or by mail from The Sacred Trinity Centre, Chapel Street, Salford.

110

8 HARVEST

To many people harvest appears as a semi-pagan, nostalgic and outmoded festival. After all, most of us do not live in rural areas where we see the fields being 'ploughed and scattered' and our appreciation of food is far removed from the images of 'seedtime and harvest'.

Yet celebration of harvest is popular in churches and schools. It has the qualities of colour and joy that children love and there is nothing wrong with encouraging children to be thankful for all that they have, particularly that most basic thing – food.

But is that all that a study of harvest has to offer? Consider all that has preceded the harvest season. There has been the resting of the land in the winter and its preparation for the seeds to be sown in the spring, followed by the growing period over the summer months. Harvest is the culmination of all these seasons. People are thankful for that, particularly in societies where the food proceeds more directly from land to mouth than it does in Britain. However disguised the links, we still depend upon good harvests as we cannot create food by artificial means, despite our sophisticated systems of processing and preserving. We are even more dependent upon the weather to ensure the successful growth of the crops, although in some rich Western societies where hydroponic farming is practised, we can create ideal weather conditions technologically. Ultimately, however sophisticated the technology, we are still at the mercy of nature. It is little wonder that ancient cultures worshipped the elements as gods.

To the people of the major religions today, God is in control of nature and it is to him that thanks are given for a successful harvest and to him that prayers are offered for future success. That is not to say that famine is natural or the result of God withholding his blessings. The recent problems in Ethiopia have political as well as natural causes.

If we look at harvest in these terms, we can see that there is a force greater than ourselves, whether you call it God or nature, and this idea is basic to all religion. Harvest, then, could be a good starting point for moving outwards from the children's experience to investigate aspects of world religions, and especially this sense of God.

Thematic approaches to harvest

The following themes can be studied throughout the year with the religious aspects of harvest being introduced at the appropriate time – at the beginning, middle or end of the project.

Harvest as a basic element in all religions

Harvest and the forces of nature could be used as an introduction to religion generally. All religions acknowledge a force greater than mankind, a force which is in control of the harvest and all that goes to make it fail or succeed. Most call that force God, though many might call it nature; this belief is common to all cultures. The Jewish festival of Sukkot and the Hindu festival of Holi celebrate the harvest, and Christians in Britain thank God each year for the harvest even though our dependence on the forces of nature is less obvious nowadays than it used to be.

The seasons

A study of harvest could follow several months of learning about seasons; weather, planting, nurturing and finally harvesting. Children could grow things in class, at home, in the school grounds. When produce is harvested will depend upon what it is and when it is sown. Something simple and quick is mustard and cress, but children could, if resources allow, be engaged in planting and growing seed potatoes, carrots, beans, plants and flowers. The school may have fruit trees or flowers in the grounds. The family of one of the children in class may have a variety of interesting vegetation. If not, why not explore the local environment? Parks and farms will be a rich resource.

There are many books on this subject and only a few are listed below. The whole project can be enriched with poetry, stories and music, such as Vivaldi's 'Four Seasons' and Delius's 'On Hearing the First Cuckoo in Spring'. The school hymn-book is a good resource here too. As well as the usual harvest hymns, there are songs like 'Morning has broken'.

Food production and manufacture

Depending on the factories near your school, you could follow the manufacturing process of certain foods. The study of food processing could be preceded by a trip to an appropriate producer. For example, the work in a flour mill (or bakery) would be traced to wheat fields, canned meat to animal rearing and the slaughterhouse. This will almost certainly also throw up the question of vegetarianism! Breeding animals for milk is another aspect to study, with visits to dairies and farms. The Milk Marketing Board may be able to supply useful leaflets.

Work on food could also incorporate discussion about diet – good and bad: school meals, vegetarianism, famine and food around the world. The latter could act as a lead into discussing the food laws or eating customs of another religion and be the starting point for a study of that religion.

Conservation

Harvest is all about taking out of the earth, but this is not possible unless we put something into the earth. The land has to be nurtured and seeds sown. To take this a stage further, we could look at other things which are taken from the earth, like oil and gas and paper from trees and consider what can be done to 'put something back'. As the American Indian Chief Seathl reportedly said in the nineteenth century: 'the earth does not belong to man, man belongs to the earth. . . . Man did not weave the web of life; he is merely a strand in it. Whatever he does to the web, he does to himself.'

We cannot overpower the earth and we cannot continue to take from it without putting anything back, say the conservationists. Just as the farmer has to nourish the soil that nourishes his crops, so too do we have to realise that the earth's resources are limited and we cannot continue to bleed those resources. We must therefore conserve what we have. Children could look at the way in which we waste things: paper bags, bottles, newspapers, packaging, etc. They could consider how these things could be re-used or recycled. There are a few interesting statistics that could be used here. Twenty per cent of the earth's population uses 80 per cent of its resources. We throw away five million tons of paper every year in Britain alone – the equivalent of 85 million trees! We, in Britain, drink our way through 3.8 billion cans of beverages. Half the cans are made from expensive aluminium which is difficult to dispose of. It could be recycled, as are over half the cans in the United States. Every year the average family uses 112 lb of metal and 90 lb of plastic. Every year in Europe alone 21,000 million tons of rubbish are dumped; 80 per cent of this could be recycled. Children could look at ways of conserving the earth's resources by using returnable bottles and bottle banks, not accepting expensive packaging and paper bags, collecting newspapers and milk-bottle tops for recycling and using biodegradable products.

The Body Shop is an example of a popular commercial enterprise that originated from a desire to produce and market conservation-conscious cosmetics. The Body Shop uses minimal packaging made from recycled paper and biodegradable plastic and all their products are biodegradable. It also offers a refill service, thus cutting down even more on the need for packaging.

USEFUL ADDRESSES

Friends of the Earth, 26-28 Underwood Street, London N1 7JG
The Conservation Society, 12 London Road, Chertsey, Surrey KT16 8AA
The Ecologist (a journal) is available from 73 Molesworth St, Wadebridge, Cornwall

Famine and famine relief

Having looked at the harvest and all that we have in this country, it might be worth considering what happens when the harvest doesn't come. The recent problems in Ethiopia have brought this into sharp focus in our sitting rooms through the medium of television. Drought, overpopulation, poor irrigation, lack of education and poor government are all reasons given as contributory causes of famine. So it can be seen that causes can be natural or man-made. Christian Aid is a charity which seeks to help the victims of famine, not only with immediate aid in the form of food and clothing, but in long-term projects of education, immunisation and irrigation. Christian Aid, OXFAM, CAFOD and other similar charities also produce literature and games for use in schools to demonstrate the causes and effects of famine. Jews and Muslims raise funds for such purposes as famine relief at festivals such as Purim and Ramadan and Eid-ul-fitr. From a Christian point of view, helping famine victims is simply an extension of Jesus's command to 'Love your neighbour'. A study of harvest and then of famine could lead to a fund-raising effort culminating in a harvest celebration.

ADDRESSES

Christian Aid (publications), P O Box 1, London SW9 8BH
CAFOD (Catholic Fund for Overseas Development), 2 Romero Close, Stockwell Road, London SW9 9TY
OXFAM, 274 Banbury Road, Oxford OX2 7DZ
World Development Movement, 26 Bedford Chambers, London WC2 8EA

The Christian celebration of Harvest

Origins

Harvest celebrations have taken place for many years in many parts of the world. They have not necessarily been religious festivals, but nature festivals celebrating the end of months of intensive labour on the land.

Harvest was an enjoyable, often rowdy feast, with plenty of cider and ale as well as food. This rowdiness led some Christian clergy in the mid-nineteenth century to try to ban the festival, while others emphasised its Christian aspect. A priest from Cornwall by the name of Hawker linked harvest home, as it was called, with a Christian Thanksgiving service in 1843. In 1857 Archdeacon George Denison of East Brent started a Christian Harvest Home feast which still continues in the same form today.

The features of the East Brent Harvest Home can be seen in many Christian harvest celebrations throughout the country. The church harvest supper was conceived as an alternative to the drunken revelling that used to be the norm. This takes place on church premises and can include dancing as well as the supper. There may be ceremonial items applauded at the supper or put on display in the church: items such as plum puddings and cheese, a huge loaf in the shape of a sheaf of corn, hoops decorated with leaves and flowers and corn dollies. Corn dollies were made because it was thought to be unlucky to cut the last sheaf of the harvest. The stems were plaited into a corn dolly while they were still growing then felled by the reapers' sickles. The dolly was dressed and decorated with garlands and carried home in a procession. It was kept all winter in the church or farmhouse to bring good luck on the next year's harvest. The custom has its roots in the pagan rites of the Middle East 7000 years ago, when people believed that the fertility goddess hid in the last sheaf of corn and needed to be appeased.

In the church services, harvest hymns such as 'We plough the fields and scatter' are sung along with the one said to have been written specially for the East Brent Harvest Home service, 'Come, ye thankful people, come'.

Most churches are also decorated with offerings of local produce which will later be distributed among the needy in the parish. Often the children bring their family offerings in gaily decorated baskets which they take up to the minister during the service. Nowadays these baskets are as likely to contain tins of baked beans and packets of tea bags as they are to contain fresh fruit and vegetables. The former are probably more practical anyway, especially if they are going to the homes of single pensioners. Even tinned they are the produce of the earth. The idea of sharing is one which might be taken up on a more global scale, considering for example whether EEC food mountains should exist while people are starving in Ethiopia.

RECIPE FOR HARVEST SUPPER

These recipes have no symbolic significance, but are typical at harvest suppers in churches today. The ingredients are natural things to use as they are part of the harvest produce.

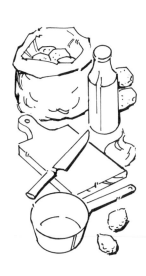

Cottage pie
1 lb minced beef
one onion
stock cube
2 lb potatoes

METHOD
Peel and boil the potatoes in a pan of water until soft. Cook the mince and chopped onion in a pan in a tablespoon of oil until browned. Add stock cube and water to cover and simmer for 30 mins. Add salt and pepper to taste. Mash the boiled potatoes with some milk and butter. Put the cooked mince into a casserole dish. Spread the potatoes on top and lightly brown the top under a grill.

Apple pie

8 oz shortcrust pastry (frozen commercially prepared pastry could be used or a packaged pastry mixture that only needs water added to it)
1½ lb apples
4 oz sugar
a little milk to glaze

METHOD

Line a 7-inch flan dish or pie plate with the pastry. Peel and slice the apples and cook in a pan with the sugar and a little water till they are soft. Pour the stewed apples onto the pastry and cover with another layer of pastry. Seal the two layers of pastry together and brush the top with milk. Prick the top with a fork to form a vent. Bake in the oven at 200°C/400°F or Mark 6 for about 30 mins.

The pie can be made using other seasonal fruit, such as damsons and plums. Crumble can be made instead of pastry. The stewed fruit is put in a flan dish or casserole dish and topped with the pastry mixture before water is added. Sprinkle with sugar and cook until the topping is golden brown.

■ TASKS

1. Make up the recipes. Hold a harvest meal.

2. Make corn dollies.

Use specially grown wheat which is long enough for this purpose. Wheat used to be grown like this, but nowadays wheat and corn are often short. Since you can only use from the ear to the first set of leaves, modern wheat will not be long enough. Before using the wheat straws, soak them for half an hour and wrap them in a damp tea-cloth. Use the straws while they are still damp so that they bend easily. If you cannot get wheat, use art-straws which can be bought from craft shops and educational suppliers. If you need to join extra straw on to your dolly, pinch the end of the piece you are working on and slot it into the hollow of the new piece.

For a basic plait, take five pieces of straw and tie them together at one end with a piece of wool. Flatten out the straws so that they point in four directions, north, south, east and two to the west. Hold the straws with your left hand and work with your right. Take the lower west straw (leader) and bend it over so that it sits above the east straw. Take the lower east straw and place it on the left of the north straw. Take the right north straw and place it on the left of the west straw, then put the west straw above the south straw and start again. You will find it easier, once you get the hang of it, to rotate the dolly in your left hand so that the action with your right is always the same. This will form a narrow plait which, when finished, can be moulded; for example, into a shepherd's crook. It will be necessary to thread a piece of wire (i.e. the sort used by florists) through the dolly to make it malleable.

To widen the dolly, place the lead straw on the outside instead of crossing it over the opposite straw, then bring the straw alongside it under the lead straw before taking it over to the opposite side. This will make a traditional horn shape. Decorate the dolly with ears of wheat or corn and ribbons. They can be painted (use thick paint with art-straws as they are so absorbent) or sprayed.

3. Read and write poetry about harvest time or the seasons or nature, depending upon the approach you have taken.

The Jewish Harvest as celebrated during Sukkot

The Jews celebrate two harvests. One in May, 50 days after Passover, which also commemorates the giving of the Law to Moses on Mount Sinai, and one in October, called Sukkot. The latter is close in time to the Christian celebrations of harvest and so is described here in detail.

The end of Sukkot with Simchat Torah (the birthday of the Law) marks the end of a cycle of festivals in the Jewish calendar, just as harvest is the culmination of the cycle of nature. Sukkot is a time of joyful thanksgiving and is a popular festival among the Jews. It was originally a time of celebration for the fruit and grape harvest and, because it fell after the harvest had been gathered, farmers were free to go to Jerusalem to celebrate it, unlike other festival times when they were unable to leave their crops.

The festival was condemned by the prophets Hosea and Amos because of the excessive drinking and eventually the Jewish leaders changed the purpose of the festival to add in a Jewish historical dimension. So the festival now also commemorates the time that the

Jews wandered in the wilderness after escaping from Egypt and had to build temporary huts or booths (*sukka*) in which to live. In the same way, the Jewish farmers used to live in huts in the fields at harvest time as their dawn to dusk work left little time for them to travel home.

Part of the celebration of Sukkot involves each Jewish family in building their own *sukkot* in the garden. This is not always possible but there is always a sukkot in each synagogue. Many Jews eat some or all of their meals in the booth during the eight days of Sukkot and some of them also sleep there. There are certain specifications for building a booth. The wooden building must be no higher than 30 feet and must have at least three walls. The roof must be made from straw and leaves and you should be able to see the stars through it. The inside is decorated with fruit and flowers and branches are laid over the roof.

There is also symbolic vegetation. *Lulav* wands are made by twisting palm, myrtle and willow branches together, as instructed in the Bible, as a sign of unity. The *etrog* is the fruit of a citron tree, rather like a lemon, which the Bible calls the 'fruit of a goodly tree'. There are various explanations of the symbolism of the lulav and etrog. One rabbinic writing says that the four plants represent the Jewish people: just as each plant has different features, so too there are good Jews and not-so-

119

good Jews, Orthodox Jews and Reform Jews, those who attend the synagogue and those who do not. They are all tied together to represent the Jewish people as a whole. Another explanation is that the priests used to process around the altar holding up the lulav and etrog, praying for rain. Rain had allowed the plants to grow and the Jews too needed rain in order to survive. This sentiment is still expressed each day of Sukkot, except for Shabbat, when the lulav and etrog are paraded around the *bimah* (platform in the synagogue) and on the seventh day the congregation parades around too. They shout 'Hoshana' ('God help us'). On the eighth day there are no lulav and etrog in the synagogue as it is a new festival, Shemini Atheret, and there is a special prayer for rain – rain that is sufficient to give good crops, but not so heavy that it causes floods. Rain in the autumn in Israel is important for irrigating the land and preparing it for the growing months. Even Jews who do not live in Israel say this prayer. Wherever in the world Jews are, they need rain, and they also care about their fellow Jews in Israel. Rain is also a symbol of God's mercy and the Jews pray that God will continue to have mercy on the world.

In any case Sukkot does not merely celebrate what has been, but what will be – the autumn rain that will come. The Jews in the wilderness lived from day to day in the makeshift booths, but they had faith in better things to come. They got their reward when they entered the Promised Land.

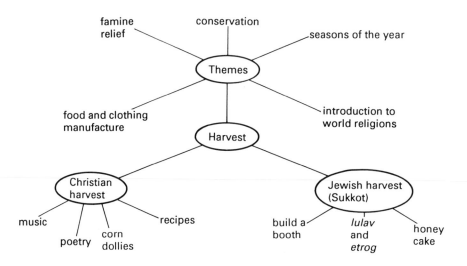

■ TASKS

1. Make up the recipe for honey cake

2. Make a lulav

3. Make and decorate a sukkot booth

Honey cake

3 eggs
1 cup sugar
2 tablespoons salad oil
3½ cups sifted flour
2 teaspoons baking powder
2 teaspoons bicarbonate of soda
½ teaspoon salt
½ teaspoon ginger
¼ teaspoon nutmeg
1 teaspoon cinnamon
dash of cloves
1 cup honey
1 cup warm coffee
½ cup chopped walnuts

METHOD

Beat eggs and sugar and stir in oil. Add dry ingredients and liquid ingredients alternately. Then stir in nuts. Turn into greased and floured round cake tin. Bake for 50 mins at 325°F or gas Mark 4. Before serving, dust with icing sugar.

121

BIBLIOGRAPHY

Christian Education Movement (2 Chester House, Pages Lane, London N10 1PR) has published a series of booklets in the Exploring a Theme series (1988). The ones on *Seasons, Harvest* and *Food* are useful here.

Althea, *The Year Around Us* (Dinosaur Books, 1982)

Jill Barklem, The Brambly Hedge Series: *Spring Story, Summer Story, Autumn Story* and *Winter Story* (Collins, 1980)

Eric Carle, *The Tiny Seed* (Hodder and Stoughton, 1987)

Usborne Book of Nature (Usborne Publishing, 1980)

Jayne Fisher, The Garden Gang Series (Ladybird, 1979 onwards)

BIBLIOGRAPHY AND ADDRESSES

General

The Concise Encyclopedia of Living Faiths (ed. R. C. Zaehner) (Hutchinson/
Open University, 1959)
The World Religions (Lion, 1982)
Derek Bastide, *Religious Education 5–12* (Falmer Press, 1987)
Leonard and Carolyn Wolcott, *Religions Around the World* (1970)

Christianity

The New International Dictionary of the Christian Church, ed. J. D. Douglas
(Paternoster, 1974)
The Oxford Dictionary of the Christian Church. ed. F. L. Cross and E. A.
Livingstone (OUP, 1974)
I. H. Birnie, *Trevor Huddleston* (People with a Purpose Series; SCM Press)
Faith in Action Series (RMEP):
    R. J. Owen, *I Wish He Were Black* (Trevor Huddleston) (1978)
    R. J. Owen, *Free at Last* (Martin Luther King) (1980)
    A. Constant, *No Compromise* (D. Bonhoeffer) (1983)

Judaism

Morris Epstein, *All about Jewish Holidays and Customs* (KTAV Publishing
House, 1959, 1970)
Harry Gersh, *When a Jew Celebrates* (Behrman House, 1971)
Vanora Leigh, *Anne Frank* (Great Lives Series; Wayland, 1985)
A. Bull, *Anne Frank* (Profiles Series; Hamish Hamilton, 1984)

Islam

Alfred Guillaume, *Islam* (Penguin, 1954, reprinted several times to 1979)
Janis Hannaford, *Ramadan and Eid-ul-fitr* (Living Festivals Series; RMEP,
1982)
Richard Tames, *Approaches to Islam* (John Murray, 1982)

Mardijah Aldrich Tarantino, *Marvellous Stories from the Life of Muhammad* (Islamic Foundation, 1986)
Ahmad Von Denffer, *Islam for Children* (Islamic Foundation, 1986)
David Wade, *The Islamic Colouring Book* (Wildwood House, 1976)

Hinduism

Olivia Bennett, *Festival! Diwali* (Commonwealth Institute/Macmillan Education, 1986) with accompanying worksheets by Rosalind Kerven.
Janis Hannaford, *Holi* (Living Festivals Series; RMEP, 1983)
V. P. (Hemant) Kanitkar, *Hinduism* (Religions of the World Series; Wayland, 1986)
Howard Marsh, *Diwali* (Living Festivals Series; Arnold Wheaton/RMEP, 1982)
K. M. Sen, *Hinduism* (Pelican, 1961)
Eric J. Sharpe, *Thinking about Hinduism* new ed. (Lutterworth, 1988)
Margaret Stutley, *Hinduism* (Aquarian Press, 1985)
Joanna Troughton, *The Story of Rama and Sita* (Blackie)
Swami Yogeshananda, *The Way of the Hindu* (Hulton Educational, 1973)

ADDRESSES

Sacred Trinity Centre, Chapel Street, Salford (for artefacts and city trails)
The Slide Centre Ltd, Ilton, Ilminster, Somerset TA19 9HS
Christian Education Movement (has publications on religions other than Christianity), 2 Chester House, Pages Lane, London N10 1PR. Also produces excellent termly magazine *R.E. Today* (editorial address 47 Prospect Park, Exeter, Devon EX4 6NA. Tel: 0392 31564)
Church Information Office, Church House, Dean's Yard, London SW1P 3NZ
Council of Christians and Jews, 1 Dennington Park House, London NW6 1AX (Tel: (071) 794 8178/9). For resources and audio-visual material.
Christian Aid (publications), PO Box 1, London SW9 8BH
CAFOD (Catholic Fund for Overseas Development), 2 Romero Close, Stockwell Road, London SW9 9TY
OXFAM, 274 Banbury Road, Oxford OX2 7DZ

The Hindu Centre, Edge Lane, Liverpool
The Hindu Centre, 39 Grafton Terrace, London NW5
Institute of Indian Culture, 44 Castletown Road, London W14 9HE

Jewish Chronicle Publications, 24 Furnival Street, London EC4A 1JT
Jewish Education Bureau, 8 Westcombe Avenue, Leeds

The Islamic Foundation Publications Unit, Unit 9, The Old Dunlop
Factory, 62 Evington Valley Road, Leicester. Tel: 0533 734860
The Islamic Foundation, 223 London Road, Leicester
The Islamic Centre, Woking Mosque, Woking, Surrey

BBC Publications (for example, notes accompanying the series 'Watch').
Tel: (081) 991 8031 (24-hour service)

INDEX

(*Italic* references are to illustrations.)

126